Praise for
***Forty Days in Italy Con La Mia Famiglia:
How to Research Your Italian Roots &
Travel to Italy on Your Own Terms***

"Anthony Fasano is living the dream! He returned to bella Italia and unearthed his glorious roots in four ancestral villages. His journey will inspire and delight you. Every Italian American and every American of immigrant descent (is that all of us?) will find much to savor here. Bravo Antonio!"

— **Adriana Trigiani,
Bestselling Author of *The Shoemaker's Wife***

"Anthony is one of those rare people who lets passion and curiosity spur him forward. As he began to learn more about his Italian-American heritage, it was inevitable the path would lead back to where it all began, and he would let none of the easy excuses—lack of time, money, language skills—stop him.

"Through fortitude and a deep, genuine desire to reconnect with his Italian roots, Anthony did what most people only dream of: he found his Italian relatives and traveled to Italy to meet them! In doing so, he's reunited the American and Italian sides of his family for future generations as no one before him was able to. And now he's giving you a guide to do the same for you and your family."

— **Dolores Alfieri,
Co-Host of The Italian American Podcast**

"In his eminently practical and deeply passionate guide to visiting Italy and discovering his extended family, The Italian-American Podcast co-host Anthony Fasano details step-by-step how to research and retrace your ancestral roots. The fruits of his efforts affirm that we never truly leave the past behind, but rather our past shapes and informs the person we become."

— **Maria Laurino,**
Author of *The Italian Americans: A History*

"My own dream of Italy was fulfilled when I visited my ancestral hometown in southern Italy in the summer of 1995 by just showing up with some names of ancestors and a few pages copied out of a local phone book which I found at the Italian Tourism Board in New York City.

"I wish there had been something like Anthony's book to guide me at the time. This is both a practical guide and a love letter to Italy and Italian-American culture. It makes the process less daunting. If you are even thinking about finding your Italian roots, get Anthony's book and make the trip—your life will be changed forever!"

— **Kathy McCabe**
Host, Dream of Italy on PBS

FORTY DAYS IN ITALY CON LA MIA FAMIGLIA

*How to Research Your Italian Roots
& Travel to Italy on Your Own Terms*

ANTHONY FASANO

FOREWORD BY CASSANDRA SANTORO,
CEO + FOUNDER OF TRAVEL ITALIAN STYLE

Forty Days in Italy Con La Mia Famiglia:
How to Research Your Italian Roots & Travel to Italy on Your Own Terms
© 2017 by Anthony Fasano

Published by Niche Content Press

All rights reserved. No portion of this book may be reproduced, stored in a retrieval system, or transmitted in any form or by any means—electronic, mechanical, photocopy, recording, scanning, or other—except for brief quotations in critical reviews or articles, without the prior written permission of the publisher.

While the author has made every effort to provide accurate internet addresses throughout the text, neither the publisher nor the author assumes any responsibility for errors, or for changes that occur after publication. Further, the author and publisher do not have any control over and do not assume any responsibility for third-party websites or their content.

ISBN-13: 978-0-9989987-5-6 (Paperback)
ISBN-13: 978-0-998-9987-1-8 (E-book)

Edited by Elisa Doucette, Craft Your Content
Cover by Robert Bridges
Interior Layout by James Woosley, FreeAgentPress.com

Dedication

To Grandpa Sal,
who died back home in the States while we
were on this forty-day journey through Italy;
we know you were there with us,
especially in Sortino, where we visited the
house your mother grew up in.

Thanks for the inspiration in writing this
book and for being there always.

Contents

Foreword xi

A Note for You xv

Introduction xvii

Part I: Dreaming, Research, Travel Planning, and Learning Italian 1

Chapter 1: Learning about Your Origins from Your Relatives 3

Chapter 2: Making the Commitment to Learn About Who You Really Are 15

Chapter 3: Understanding your Origins and Finding Your Family in Italy 21

Chapter 4: Learning the Beautiful Italian Language 41

Chapter 5: Planning the Trip of a Lifetime to Italy 57

Part II: The Trip of a Lifetime 81

Chapter 6: Italy — Arrival & Acclimation 83

Chapter 7: The Eternal City and the Amalfi Coast 99

Chapter 8: La Mia Famiglia 121

Chapter 9: Sicilia Here we Come 147

Chapter 10: Great-Great-Grandma Rosina's Home of Sortino ... 161

Chapter 11: The Beginning, or the End? 175

Acknowledgments 181

About the Author 183

Foreword

Growing up in a Sicilian-American family, my father frequently played the 1993 ESPN speech by the legendary Italian American basketball coach Jimmy Valvano. The part of the speech that always stood out the most to me was Jimmy's advice for success:

"To think about what's important in life, to me, are these three things: where you started, where you are, and where you're going to be."

This idea stayed with me from my late teens on, especially after the loss of my father.

About three years after my father's passing, I embarked on a journey to Italy to discover my roots and to learn where my family really started. I began slowly, traveling throughout Italy and Sicily. I began doing genealogical research and applying for dual citizenship. I knew I wanted to hold on to my beautiful Italian memories as long as possible. I wanted to know about my grandparents, their parents, and all that shaped us as

Italian Americans. I knew this journey was the only way I could discover who I was and where I wanted to be.

It took almost a decade of living back and forth between Italy and New York, conducting hours of personal research, hiring dozens of genealogy professionals, and staring at my bank accounts thousands of dollars later, until I proudly held my Italian passport as a dual citizen and could claim with confidence that I knew the history of my family.

Shortly after completing this journey, I launched a company specializing in Italian travel. It wasn't long until I introduced the concept of family history travel through custom Italian Heritage Trips. In collaboration with expert genealogists, local historians, and Italian archeologists, my company researches the family history of our clients and creates a tour of the region where the family originated. We walk them through churches where their parents married, bakeries their grandparents worked in, or simply spend time explaining the local culture and history in depth while strolling the streets of their family town.

When I met Anthony and he told me about his family history adventure and documentation of his process, I could be nothing but inspired and awed! Anthony's journey gives you the tools to discover the past. You will be able to open the door to the lives that shaped you and embark on an unforgettable personal journey, one that you can share with generations to come.

We are all excited to see where your own family research may lead you — perhaps one step of your journey will include a family heritage trip to Italy. No matter what, don't forget where you started, where you are, or where you're going to be.

As Anthony and I discovered, beautiful things can emerge from remembering where you come from!

Con i migliori auguri

*— **Cassandra Santoro**
CEO + Founder of Travel Italian Style*

A Note for You...

This book has two distinct parts. Part I contains specific instructions as to how you can locate your living Italian relatives or simply learn more about your Italian ancestors. Part II is an account of my own 40-day trip to Italy with my family of five, where I met my living Italian relatives for the first time and started to build beautiful relationships.

It is my hope that you use this book to get the most out of your Italian American experience; believe me—it can be an amazingly rich one.

Additional photos and information from my trip, as well as information on how you can take your own trip, can be accessed through my website for this book, FortyDaysInItaly.com. There is also a special travel planning document that you can use to plan your trip on the book website.

Introduction

I was running as fast as I could, pulling two wheeled suitcases, constantly looking back to make sure the rest of my family was close behind. My 10-year-old daughter Brianna was right behind me, running swiftly with two bags. My seven-year-old son AJ was close behind her, a look of terror on his face, and my wife Jill was last in line, pushing the stroller carrying our four-year-old, Penelope and running as fast as she could.

We were in the midst of the first leg of a long trip from our humble abode in New Jersey to the home of our ancestors (and some new-found living relatives) in Italy.

The first stop of what would be an unforgettable 40-day journey was set to be Lerici in northwestern Italy, close to Le Cinque Terre, but it was a long and complicated 24 hours of travel to get there. Especially with a family of five.

We were in the Florence train station, and had arrived at Track 18, from where we thought our 1 p.m. train was about to leave, only to realize at 12:57 that we had misread the board—our train was on Track 1A. I immediately started sprinting and the rest of the family followed.

My poor son AJ, who has anxiety, was crying throughout the entire sprint, but there was no time to stop and console him. As I ran, I was asking everyone I passed where this mysterious Track 1A was.

We found it, but just as we arrived at the train, before we could get on, the doors closed.

I stopped, my mind invaded by terrible thoughts of sitting in the station for hours with three young, upset, and tired children. Suddenly, a woman standing on the platform who had seen us running, walked up to the train and pushed a button.

The doors opened, and my wife and I looked at each other with a look that screamed, "We made it." We all smiled, thanked the woman, and climbed aboard. As we unloaded our luggage and found seats, the dryness in my throat and tightness in my calves became more apparent. I sat down and tried to gather myself.

Little did I realize that the emotional roller coaster we had experienced over the last 15 minutes was only a small sampling of what the next 40 days would hold.

From the planning stages—which included connecting with living relatives through research and learning the Italian language—to our very early flight from

Napoli Airport back to New Jersey on day 40, the whole trip was truly an amazing experience.

I am excited to bring you along on our journey through the pages of this book, and in doing so, provide you with a blueprint (and hopefully some inspiration) for taking your own once-in-a-lifetime trip.

Andiamo (We go)...

— ***Anthony Fasano***

PART I:
Dreaming, Research, Travel Planning, and Learning Italian

CHAPTER 1

Learning about Your Origins from Your Relatives

I can't type fast enough as my 86-year-old grandmother rattles off our entire family history, sentence after sentence. As my fingers fly across the keys, I'm trying to correctly spell the names of the people and places without missing other critical pieces of information.

She gives me her parents and grandparents' names, along with their dates of birth and death. She tells me the villages they were from in Italy and the stories of how and why they came to the United States.

It is all fascinating information, and the entire time I am asking myself two questions internally. Firstly, why haven't I asked her for this information before? Secondly, what if I had never asked her for it?

I leave Nonna's that day with more information than I could have imagined and an excitement about my heritage that I haven't felt before, all because I asked.

Grandma Jo's kitchen table — Nanuet, NY
Fall 2014

The Desire to Know Where I Came From

It wasn't until my mid-30s that I really started thinking about where I came from. I don't mean where I grew up; I mean where my family came from, generations earlier.

I had known I was 100 percent Italian for my entire life. The loud Sunday dinners with over 40 people gave it away, along with a hundred other traditions.

I grew up with my parents and two brothers in the small town of Suffern, in Rockland County, New York — the suburbs of New York City. We were a typical Italian-American family: hard-working parents, close-knit family traditions, and regular large family gatherings.

As much as my father used to talk about his grandfather, Antonio Fasano, who was a hard-working immigrant barber, I never thought much of it.

Then one day it hit me. I was 35 years old, thinking about my past and my family, and I decided it would be nice to really understand where in Italy my family was from. Actually, it would be nice to learn anything about the immigrants in my family, who came to the United States and gave me the life I have today.

Soon after, I had another realization, but this one was much scarier. The four people who held the key to my past were getting older, and the window for accessing this invaluable information was closing quickly. As lucky as I was to be 35 years old and still have four grandparents alive, they were getting older and not as sharp as they used to be.

So one day I called my Grandma Josephine, known within the family as Grandma Jo. She was the only one of my grandparents who I distinctly remember speaking Italian when I was younger. I asked her if I could come over for lunch and ask her some questions about our family history. Anyone who knows Italian grandmothers will know what her answer was.

Grandma's Kitchen Table

As I walked up the stairs to her apartment, laptop under my arm, I felt like I was about to uncover a treasure that I should have started looking for years ago.

She had warm eggplant parmigiana and a loaf of Italian bread on the table—the perfect way to start the afternoon. We enjoyed the lunch with my Grandpa Serafino (Sal), and then he retired to the television to watch his game shows, and my grandmother and I began to delve into our past.

I opened my laptop and used a note-taking program called Evernote to capture the information that Grandma Jo began to share. She focused on her parents and my Grandpa Sal's parents, one at a time, going through what she knew of all four of them.

She didn't just give me the hard, factual information

that I would need to dig deeper. She also told me stories about my ancestors and stories about growing up in an immigrant neighborhood, which was really powerful. I started to understand the odds that my great-grandparents were up against when they traveled on a boat from Italy to a country they knew nothing about.

They had no money. They couldn't speak the language. They didn't even know if they would survive the trip overseas. However, they all had a common goal. They wanted a better life for their families.

With every story she told, I became more and more thankful for the life I had, realizing that success hadn't just been handed to my family. It was the product of hard work, day after day, putting family above all else. This is the Italian American philosophy—*Prima la Famiglia* (Family First).

This feeling was worth more then all of the facts that I gained while sitting at Grandma's kitchen table that day. My Great-Grandpa Giuseppe had collected junk and sold it to feed his children, and my Great-Grandma Rosa had done seamstress work whenever she could to bring in money. These were the invaluable, almost-lost stories that I could now pass down to my children.

As I will share with you later in the book, it was only the beginning. With this information, I was able to find much more on my own, which culminated in visits to my great-grandparents' original villages in Italy. You can make this journey into your own heritage, too.

A Glimpse into What I Learned from that Conversation

This was just the first learning session with my Grandma, but I would go on to have many more over the next few years, and still do to this day. I want to share with you some of my notes from those visits in this section, to give you some insight into the type of information that you might search for. At the end of this chapter, I will give you some specific questions you might consider asking.

> Giuseppe Baselice, WW1 Veteran (fought for U.S.)
>
> Born: February 7, 18XX
>
> Died: 3/28/1984
>
> Born in Sarno, Italy, province of Salerno (Salerno is near Naples)
>
> Mom: Vittoria Balestrino
>
> Father: Aniello Baselice
>
> He had two sisters: Rose Baselice, Michelena Baselice
>
> Notes: Both of his parents were killed in 1943, in the Battle of Salerno in World War II. Grandma Jo remembers when the letter was delivered, a white envelope with black border; he immediately knew there was a death in the family. He was a salvage dealer (junk man). He used to go into apartments and get old newspapers from the superintendents. He used to lie and tell them he only had a certain amount of money. He gave them that much and kept the rest. He had a horse

and wagon and used it to transport the papers. He met a prosperous Italian man named Pasquala Giordano, who said to Giuseppe , "If I buy you a truck, you trade only for me." And that's what he did. They were very poor. After World War I he couldn't get a job. Fiorello LaGuardia gave him a job. An English-speaking friend of Giuseppe wrote Mayor LaGuardia a letter, and told him that a friend of his (Giuseppe) was a World War I veteran with five kids, had no job, and his kids were hungry. On Thanksgiving Eve, the Mayor sent his staff to their apartment to give them baskets of food and offer a job to Giuseppe. They never forgot that day.

Recording Memories for Future Generations

After that initial lunch with my grandmother in the fall of 2014, I sat down with her a few more times. Then, of course, life got in the way. It was now July 2015, I had experienced some success in my career creating, hosting, and building podcasts, and I was at a conference in Texas called Podcast Movement.

If you are not familiar with podcasts, a podcast is a digital audio file, published on the Internet for downloading to a computer or portable media player. It is typically available as a series, and new installments can be accessed by subscribers automatically. Essentially, a podcast is an on-demand radio show.

My podcasts at the time were all focused on engineering and science. I was sitting in the audience, listening to one of the conference keynote speakers, an Italian-American named Lou Mongello. He was talking about how important it is to be yourself as the host of a podcast, as this will allow you to really connect with your audience, and letting your passion for the topic shine through, episode after episode.

Now even though I had slowed down a bit on my family research, the passion to dig deeper was still there. I wanted to do more than just learn about my family history, I wanted to preserve it for future generations. These thoughts of my Italian heritage and preserving it were constantly popping up in my mind when I first had the idea: **The Italian-American Podcast**. What a perfect way to record and preserve my family history.

At the next break, I ran up to my hotel room and purchased ItalianAmericanPodcast.com, which has since been changed to ItalianAmericanExperience.com. Later that evening, I sketched out the initial plan for the show. The initial plan was built around the idea that I would visit my grandparents more often, record their stories, and include these stories as episodes so that years from now, my children and their children could listen to them.

As planning for the podcast progressed, I was fortunate to convince a long-time family friend, Dolores Alfieri, to co-host with me. In fact, there was no convincing needed, just one simple phone call. Dolores is a first-generation Italian-American—both of her parents immigrated to the United States.

I know Dolores well because she is related to my sister-in-law and grew up in the same small town that I did. I also knew that she had dedicated a few years of her life to writing a memoir about growing up Italian-American.

I felt like things were starting to come together with my family research. I now had many hard facts from my grandmother, as well as some stories on audio, and the podcast offered a tangible way to record it.

Before we move on to my next step which focuses on the commitment required for this journey, I want to leave you with some questions that you can use when having these critical conversations with your relatives about your family history. You will find sections like this at the end of most chapters, designed to help you take action on planning your own amazing family journey.

ACTION ITEMS FOR YOU:
Questions to Ask Your Relatives

While I am passionate about writing, writing doesn't mean as much to me if my readers don't take measurable action in their own lives. I've added these sections at the end of most chapters to provide either action items to help in your own endeavors, or lessons that I learned during my journey. This should help you to ensure that you don't make the same mistakes.

I want to inspire you to dig deeper into your family history, starting with talking with any living relatives that may be able to help you. The questions below are phrased in a manner so you can literally read them off, one-by-one, at the table.

1. What was the last name of all of my great-grandparents or my relatives that immigrated to the U.S. from Italy?

You can start with your grandparents and work backwards. I was lucky to easily find seven out of eight of my great-grandparents' surnames.

2. What village in Italy did our family originate from?

This is a critically important question. If you know this or can obtain this answer, then at a minimum you can visit the village and start to understand where you really came from. You might even find living relatives, or at least people who know your family, by mentioning the last names.

3. What are the birth years of my great-grandparents or my relatives that immigrated to the U.S. from Italy?

This is another critically important piece of information. If you have both the village of origin and birth year of one of your relatives, you can most likely obtain or view their birth certificate by visiting the village. More on this in Chapter 2.

4. What are the death years of my great-grandparents or other relatives that never immigrated to the US?

If you know of a relative who was born and died in Italy, and have both the village of origin and death year of that person, you can likely obtain or view their death certificate by visiting the village, which has a lot of detailed information. More on this in Chapter 2.

5. What year did our family members immigrate to the U.S.?

If you can figure this out, you can attempt to find the manifest of the ship that they came to the U.S. aboard by searching online.

These questions will get you started with your research and help to you find some of the most critical information for finding the records of your family. You can download these questions, and find other helpful resources, at FortyDaysInItaly.com.

These hands-on tools and guidelines can all be very helpful in your research, but next I made a decision that would supercharge the research into my family history and heritage, way beyond the choice of the physical tools that I used.

CHAPTER 2

Making the Commitment to Learn About Who You Really Are

As I delve deeper into the research of my family history (or as I think of it: where I came from), it is obvious to me that the best way to really connect with my past is to go back to where my ancestors came from. I need to visit the villages they were born in. I need to see the streets they played in as children. I need to taste the food that they tasted.

But how can I do this? This will require an extended trip to Italy, which will be rather difficult for a young family of five.

Then my wife and I made a decision that would ultimately change everything.

Sitting on my back porch — Bergen County, NJ
Late Summer 2015

The Decision to do Something Really Scary (and Why You Should Go for It)

At this point in the process, doubt started creeping into my mind. Was finding and visiting relatives in Italy even possible? Was it worth my time? With multiple businesses and three children, I couldn't afford to waste years of my life researching, only to find nothing.

By now, it was late summer of 2015, and I needed to either give up or make a serious commitment to seeing this through; if I kept doubting myself, nothing good was going to happen. I had waited too long in my life to start the research process, and although I had progressed in leaps and bounds since that first lunch meeting with my grandmother, there was still a long road ahead.

It was during this summer that I decided to commit to what, for some, might seem unthinkable.

We weren't quite sure where we would go, or how we would pay, but after discussing it with my wife, we decided that we would take a lengthy, multi-week trip to Italy the following summer (2016). Most Americans in their thirties with young kids envision a trip like this being attainable only once they are retired, not while they are in the prime of their careers.

Once we'd made this decision, I was inspired to focus on maximizing the experience in Italy, and really making it happen.

Making the Commitment to Learn About Who You Really Are

I have realized in life that the greatest success comes when I do things that I am afraid of, that feel completely uncomfortable. People refer to this as moving outside of your comfort zone, and that was definitely true of this trip for my wife and me. Think about it. I was thirty-six years old, living a good life as an Italian-American in a middle-class area of a very nice neighborhood in the United States. My wife and I had very little savings at the time, and didn't even know if we had living relatives in Italy. My three children, who I mentioned in the introduction, hadn't really travelled at all, beyond the two-hour car ride to the Jersey shore we made once a summer. What on earth made us think we could pull this off?

But I thought back to my great-grandparents, who risked their lives by leaving their homes behind and getting on a boat to a country where they couldn't speak the language, and which they weren't even sure if they would be allowed into. Maybe it was their courage that inspired me to make my own voyage go from dream to reality.

My wife and I had studied abroad together in college. We spent a semester in Brussels, Belgium, and while we were there, we visited thirteen different countries, including Italy. I distinctly remember other students at school telling us that we couldn't leave campus for six months, as we would miss out on the crazy beer parties. Seriously? Thankfully, we didn't listen, and the trip was amazing.

That trip to Brussels was my first trip outside of the U.S., other than a few trips to Canada, and it made my wife and I realize that there was an entire world out there beyond our home. It exposed us to different cultures, languages, and food; and it got us interested in travel.

If you haven't had that first international travel experience yet, don't be discouraged. Now is the best time to do it. You have no idea what you are missing. As you will read about in this book, we made a ton of mistakes on this trip, proving that your first family travel experience may not be the easiest, but can still produce life-changing memories.

I was also spurred on by my Uncle Carl's 60th birthday celebration plans. My Uncle Carl has always celebrated milestone birthdays with a trip of some sort, which brings him the best present of all: time together with his family, away from everyday life. He had been talking for years about celebrating his 60th birthday in a villa in Sicily, with our family. My grandfather's family was from Sicily, and I had heard from other family members that there were still living relatives there.

Knowing that my Uncle Carl and Aunt Marie were planning this trip made the decision for my wife and me easier. If we were going to take the kids all the way to Sicily for a week, it made sense to stay longer in Italy—as long as we could.

I mean, the villa that my aunt and uncle booked was one hour away from the village my great-grandparents were from. If that wasn't the perfect opportunity to capitalize on the genealogy research that I had started, what would be?

As my trip unfolds in the following pages, you'll see just how amazing an experience it ended up being, and all because we made this uncomfortable decision. So if you are considering diving deeper into your Italian family research (or any other endeavor, for that matter) but have yet to commit to it, I encourage you to go for it. Commit to doing it in a way that might be really uncomfortable for you, as I have found that the biggest risks in life pay the biggest rewards, whether events end up the way you imagined or not.

The Importance of a Goal

Once my wife and I committed to taking the trip to Italy in the summer of 2016, it became a personal goal of mine to make this trip the best it could possibly be. I knew it could be a once-in-a-lifetime trip and I wasn't going to take it for granted.

Over the next year, I spent hours planning and preparing for every facet of this trip. The travel logistics for

40 days with three children, which you'd think would have been the most complicated part of the planning, was only the beginning. I wanted to find out if I really did have living relatives in Italy, and I wanted to find them *before* I left. I wanted to learn Italian so I could really connect with people while I was there. I wanted to learn as much as I could about my great-grandparents and their birth villages, which I planned to visit.

You must have a goal with a specific deadline if you want to achieve big things in your life. Maybe you purchased this book because you have been saying for years that you want to learn more about your Italian ancestors. Well, talk is cheap; you need to make a bigger commitment.

I can't tell you what that is for you, but it doesn't have to be a full-fledged tour of Italy. It could start with a paid subscription to a genealogy website. It should be something that will inspire in you a meaningful and binding commitment to this goal.

Now that I have emphasized the importance of commitment in this journey that is family history research, let's get back to my researching story: it's time to dig into the process I used to find my family members in Italy.

CHAPTER 3

Understanding Your Origins and Finding Your Family in Italy

I can't believe it. All of my hard work has paid off. I have spent the last few years talking to family members and then researching our family origins online.

I found a website that helped me to obtain mailing addresses for houses of people with my great-grandparents' surnames in their ancestral villages. I typed letters in Italian using an online translator explaining who I was and that I was trying to find living relatives in my great-grandparents' ancestral villages. I sent them off and on a whim, included my Facebook profile URL.

And now it's happened. I've received a Facebook friend request from Maria Rosa Salese. The request comes with a message in Italian that, when translated, says: I received the letter you sent to my Uncle Francesco in Albanella. Do you know anyone in this photo?

She has attached a photo, which shows my grandmother's sister and her husband, who visited Maria Rosa and her family's farm in the mountains eight years ago. Confirmation.

I can't believe it. Maria Rosa's great-grandfather was the brother of my great-grandfather. Contact with living relatives. As I stare at her message and the photo, all I can think is "I did it!" But this is only the beginning...

Staring at my laptop in my office — **Bergen County, NJ**
Fall 2015

Two Sides of Family History Research: The Facts and the Story

Let me start this chapter by saying that I am NOT a professional genealogist, but most likely, neither are you. Therefore, you should have access to the same tools I used to track down my living relatives in Italy, and in this chapter I will walk you through the process I used.

Also, for your knowledge, in doing research for this book, I discovered that the terms *Family History* and *Genealogy* were once upon a time viewed differently. In June of 2013, Wikipedia decided to merge the pages for the two terms together and define them as the study of family lineage and history.

I want to start on this topic by talking about the two sides of family history research. In my own experience researching my family history, I felt like I was constructing two separate cases, which were nevertheless completely intertwined.

The first side of the story was the factual side. As I mentioned in Chapter 1, I collected important factual information about my relatives like birth dates, village names, and immigration dates. These facts allowed me to find certain documentation online, which was very real. For example, my great-grandfathers Antonio and Giuseppe's draft cards, which they filled out on their own. This was an amazing find for me, and again, I will show you how I did it.

My Great-Grandfather Giuseppe Baselice's draft registration card. Interestingly enough, he spelled his last name different from the way my grandmother ended up spelling it.

My Great-Grandfather Antonio Fasano's draft registration card.

As gratifying as it is to find hard data and records, the other side of family history research is just as rewarding, if not more. I am referring to your family's story. You can find all of the hard data and records imaginable, but if you really want to understand what your family went through, and what made you who you are today, you'll need to dig deeper. You will need to go beyond the records. This step is part of what made this a truly remarkable journey for me. I now realize that this is what I set out to do, discover my family story.

Factual Ancestral Research

Let's start with the facts. As I mentioned earlier, the best place to start your family history research is speaking to your relatives. I started with my grandparents and obtained any factual data that I could. I specifically worked through the questions that I listed at the end of Chapter 1. I was also able to get, from my grandparents, copies of a few birth certificates, and the marriage certificates of my great-grandparents.

Once I had this information, I started doing online research through a genealogy website. There are so many of them out there. I used Ancestry.com, which worked very well for me, but people I know have had success with other websites as well.

Through this website, I was able to search for records by inputting the information I knew. For example, I would enter the name, birth year, and birth location of my great-grandfather, and it would return any records that matched those fields. Now, of course, there are multiple Giuseppe Baselices who lived at the time of my great-grandfather, but the more facts you know, the more you can hone in on the person you are looking for.

The other piece of information that can help you ferret out your relatives amongst others with the same name, is the year they arrived in the United States. Often on these genealogy websites, the ship manifests come up in the search results. There are usually multiple manifests, again due to the number of similar names. When you build up enough facts, it becomes possible to decipher which records belong to your family members.

If you are searching in the Northeastern United States, and the genealogy website you are using doesn't return the manifest, you can search LibertyEllisFoundation.org. While many immigrants arrived through Ellis Island, and either stayed in New York or traveled from there, others entered through Baltimore, Boston, Philadelphia, New Orleans, and other U.S. ports. I list all of the websites that I used at the end of this chapter.

Doing the factual research requires a lot of time, because every record that you find needs special attention. For example, the ship manifest might give you so much information that you can then use to start to build a story, like an ancestor's occupation or where they resided on the ship coming over. Were they in an upper-class cabin, or in steerage (the lowest cargo area of the ship)? We'll talk more about this in the next section, but for now you want to collect as many records as you can.

Here are some records that I found online that proved helpful:
- Ship manifests and passenger records.
- War draft cards.
- Census information.
- Naturalization records.
- Immigration records.

Most of these genealogy sites allow you to download the records, so you can hold onto them even if you eventually decide to cancel your subscription to the website. They also allow you to build a family tree online and attach the specific records to each person in the file.

The more facts you can obtain from your family, the more success you will have in your online research efforts. Finding these records was a very special step in this process for me because it gave me tangible items that connected me to my past—which is one of the most exciting parts of doing this kind of research.

Painting a Real Picture of Where You Came From

Gathering the factual data about your Italian relatives is a critical first step to learning about your past. Once you've done that, you can start to paint the full picture of your past—the picture of who you really are and who you came from.

Think of yourself as the director of a movie all about your past, leading up to who you are today. The way you are going to make the movie is by putting all the pieces that you've found together. In doing so, you are going to add that creative and descriptive touch so the movie becomes interesting. It becomes a story people want to watch.

Let me start with my great-grandfather, Giuseppe Baselice. Again, here's the information my grandmother was able to give me:

Giuseppe Baselice, WWI Veteran (fought for U.S.)

Born: February 7, 18XX

Died: 3/28/1984

Born in Sarno, Italy, province of Salerno (Salerno is near Naples)

Mom: Vittoria Balestrino

Father: Aniello Baselice

He had two sisters: Rose Baselice, Michelena Basilice

His parents were killed in the Battle of Salerno in 1943

As I researched online I was able to find find and verify more information, including:

Born: February 7, 18XX

Arrived to U.S.: March 17, 1914

The draft card that I shared with you earlier confirmed that he had been a junk dealer, as my grandmother had said. Later on in the book, I discuss my trip to Great-Grandpa Giuseppe's hometown of Sarno, Italy, where I would obtain his actual birth certificate, which gave me some more information. There I would also confirm that his parents were killed in the battle of Salerno in 1943.

This prompted me to read a book on the battle of Salerno to gather more information for the "movie" I was creating.

Here is the excerpt again from the notes I had taken of my grandmother's memories:

> Both of his parents were killed in the Battle of Salerno in World War II [1943]. Grandma Jo remembers when the letter came in a white envelope with a black border. He [Giuseppe] immediately knew there was a death in the family. He was a salvage dealer (junk man). He used to go into the apartments and get the newspapers from the superintendents. He used to lie to the supers and tell them they had X amount of money. He gave them that much and kept the rest. He had a horse and wagon and used them to transport the papers. He met a prosperous Italian man and that man was Pasquala Giordano, and he said to Giuseppe, "If I buy you a truck, you trade only

for me." And that's what he did. They were very poor. After WWI they couldn't get a job. Mayor Fiorello LaGuardia gave him a job. An English-speaking friend wrote a letter to the mayor at the time saying he had a friend who was a World War I veteran with five children and no job and his children were hungry. On the evening of Thanksgiving, the Mayor's staff came to the house and brought baskets of food for the family and a job for Giuseppe. They never forgot that day.

You can see the story I can start to write about Great-Grandpa Giuseppe. He was born in Sarno in 1891, where Vittoria Balestrino and Aniello Basilice raised him and his two sisters, Rose and Michelena. They were raised on a farm (I know this because on the ship manifest he indicated "farm lad" as his occupation). Due to poor conditions (based on what my grandmother told me), on March 3, 1914, Giuseppe took a leap of faith, boarded a ship from Napoli, and immigrated to the United States of America at 26 years old.

He left behind everything he knew to try to create a better future for himself and his family. The ship's manifest tells us he took the leap by himself—no one else from his family came on the same ship.

It took two weeks for the ship to make it to the U.S., and he arrived here on March 17, 1914. He lived in a small Italian immigrant neighborhood in Manhattan, where he would meet my grandmother Maria Paciullo, also from Sarno, and they would get married on October 30, 1921. They would move to the Bronx, where they would have six children and raise their family. Giuseppe loved baseball. He used to go to Yankee Stadium for fifty cents, with a hero sandwich and a bottle of wine, and sit in the bleachers. He was a great bocce player. He used to take the family to Long Beach on Long Island and do hayrides. They used to cook and bring Italian food everywhere.

This is just the beginning of the story. I have since been able to gather more and more information from my grandmother, hearing different stories that continue to intrigue me and add more depth to the story I am writing. When I got the chance to visit Sarno, which I detail later in the book, it essentially gave my entire story more of a 3D feel.

My point here is that the facts of your family history are critical to your research and should be its cornerstone; however, they are only a foundation to build upon, and build you should. You should render the story of your family as vividly as you can, both for yourself and for future generations.

Reaching Out to Italy

At this point it was late summer 2015, about a year after that first lunch at my grandmother's apartment, and I had a lot of information about most of my eight great-grandparents. It was time for me to start thinking about connecting with my family in Italy. I had heard from other family members that we still had living relatives there, but the information on those relatives was very limited.

I had heard of two very distinct connections in Italy, and had confirmed these through my research.

My great-grandmother Rosina Blancato (my maternal grandfather's mother) was born in Sortino in the region of Siracusa, Sicily. She had three sisters and one brother, all of whom immigrated to the United States, **except** for her oldest sister Alfia. This was a big exception, because it meant there were the most likely living relatives in Sicily from Alfia's family. I had heard that my mother's cousin Roseanne had visited with them, but I knew nothing more of the trip.

On my father's side, I had learned that his mother's father, Germano Salese, had grown up on a farm in Albanella, in the region of Campania, Italy. Great-Grandpa Germano immigrated to the United States in September 1907. His two brothers came to the United States as well, but one of them, Angelo, didn't like it and returned to Albanella to work on the family farm. I had heard that my father's aunt visited the farm about eight years ago, but I knew nothing beyond that.

First, I reached out to my mother's cousin Roseanne and asked her about the family in Sicily. She had a lot of information that confirmed my factual research, which she shared with me. She also gave me two key pieces of information that would eventually help me make the connection with living relatives in Italy.

Roseanne had visited Sortino, Sicily on a recent trip, but she was only able to spend about an hour there. She did, however, get the email address of the son of our relative's neighbor. He was a thirty year-old computer engineer named Sebastiano who spoke English. This was a critical factor in me being able to connect, since my relatives spoke very little English and I didn't know their exact mailing address.

When trying to connect and communicate with people in southern Italy and Sicily, you must be prepared to work very hard. They often speak little English and have limited internet access, if any. I didn't realize this until after my trip. Had Roseanne not introduced me to Sebastiano, I may never have connected with my family in Sicily.

Sebastiano was extremely gracious and responsive, and his English was great. He was able to give me the exact address of my relative Nunzia, who is the equivalent in age to my mother. Her mother and my mother shared the same great-grandmother, Margherita Bucello. In about a year, I would be standing at Margherita's grave with Nunzia.

Sebastiano passed a few messages on to Nunzia for me, and also was kind enough to visit the local Comune and get a printout of my family's genealogy in Sortino. This was a huge step in my journey.

The second piece of information that Roseanne gave me was a photo. The photo was my great-grandmother Rosina with her two sisters, her late sister's daughter, and a baby who would later make this photo a very important piece of my family history puzzle.

My Great-Grandma Rose with her sisters and great-niece in Sicily in the late 1970's. Grandma Rose is on the far right and her Great-Niece Francy is on the far left.

As I mentioned, my father's aunt had visited our family in the Campania region of Italy, near Naples, about eight years ago. She lives in Florida, but it just so happened during the time I was doing my research that she came up to stay with my grandmother for one month. She told me all about her trip to Italy, and gave me enough information in the way of names and rough addresses that I was able to hone in on the exact village in which the family's farm was located. Again, the simple act of talking to my relatives proved to be very fruitful.

At this point, I felt like I had enough information to reach out directly to Italy. So I opened my laptop late one night and started typing letters to the different family members whose names I had gotten from Roseanne and my father's Aunt Faita. I found a website that allowed me to enter in their names and villages in Italy and obtain mailing addresses (see the resources section at the end of this chapter). After finishing the letters, I used Google Translate to translate them into Italian, and put them in the mail the next day.

Honestly, when I dropped the letters in the mail, I thought to myself, "I am dropping these letters into a black hole and they will never return, but at least I can say I tried."

Within 45 days of dropping those letters in the mailbox, I received two Facebook friend requests. One of those requests was from Maria Rosa Salese, from the family farm in Albanella. She said she received my letter, and she sent me a photo of my Aunt Faita and her husband on the farm, asking me if I knew these people. Confirmation. The second request came from Francesca Pagliaro (Francy). Francy was Nunzia's daughter from Sortino, Sicily. But more importantly, remember the photo I shared earlier in this section of Rosina, her sisters, and her great-niece? Well, that baby in the photo was this same Francy that just connected with me. Confirmation.

When you do family history research, these are the moments you are aiming for. Moments where you can sit back and say, "Wow." Moments where pieces of the puzzle start to fit together, and you really start to understand where you came from. You start to realize that there was, and maybe is, a whole other face of your family on the other side of the world.

I now had contact with my Italian relatives, and my Italian-American experience would be changed forever.

Communicating with My New-Found Family

Over the next few months, I would start to get acquainted with my relatives in Italy. There were times when I would spend an hour back and forth in a Facebook chat conversation, catching up on what seemed like hundreds of lost years.

It wasn't just the conversations that were thrilling to me. It was seeing their posts. Seeing the way they lived. Seeing their neighborhoods and those of other family members in their posts. Slowly, other relatives in Italy heard about us, and they also started to connect with me. I felt like I was re-assimilating into my true Italian roots. I felt like I was really starting to fully embrace my Italian-American experience.

I had achieved what many Italian Americans dream of: finding living Italian relatives. Actually, I had achieved only one part of the dream in finding them; I was still working on the second part of the dream—visiting them.

ACTION ITEMS FOR YOU:
Family Research Tools

You've just read about how I used word of mouth and the Internet to find my living relatives in Italy. Below is a list of some of the specific resources I used during this process. Please note that many times Italian-Americans have no knowledge of living family in Italy, but they frequently do exist. It is my hope that you may be able to find them using the resources listed below, but you may have to make a trip to your origin villages, which I will discuss later on in the book.

1. Speak to your older relatives.

This is the most important action you can take, more important than any website you can visit. Talk to anyone in your family who remembers past generations, and record everything they tell you. This information may come in handy when you move to online research. When you think you have talked to everyone in your family, try to find more people, whether they are distant cousins or anyone else you can get in touch with. The questions at the end of Chapter 1 will help you get the most out of these conversations.

2. Seek old photos of any kind.

Along the lines of the previous point, when you speak to elder relatives, always ask for photos. Photos can really bring your story to life. They can also serve to provide verification, like the two photos my Italian relatives and I were able to use to confirm our relationship. Remember the saying "a picture is worth a thousand words." In this case, it may be worth even more.

3. Start your online research.

Find a good genealogy research website. I used Ancestry.com, and it was and has been excellent, but there is a monthly fee of about twenty dollars. For me, it has been worth it. I mentioned some of the amazing documents that I found, including my great-grandfather's draft card, which allowed me to see his handwriting and his profession. There are many websites out there now, so select the one that works best for you.

4. Make the connection to Italy.

As you start to gain factual data, look for any possible connections to Italy, whether they be a relative who has visited there before, or online registries that allow you look for Italian citizens by name and location. I used this Italian directory website to find my relatives' addresses: http://www.paginebianche.it.

5. Reach out to your family in Italy.

Once you have addresses, you can write letters to your family in Italy. Be sure to include multiple ways to contact you, including your Facebook profile URL.

6. Build a relationship with your family.

Should your Italian relatives connect with you, get to know them. Talk to them (using Google Translate if necessary), and start to really understand where you came from.

You can download a list of these action items, and find other helpful resources, at FortyDaysInItaly.com.

All of this research and communication with Italian relatives is much easier if you can speak Italian. Do not worry, I couldn't speak Italian when I started, but during the process I learned. How? I was hoping you'd ask; that's what we're going to cover in the next chapter.

Chapter 4

Learning the Beautiful Italian Language

I am doing it. At this point, I've found so much information about my ancestors—even more excitingly, I've connected with living relatives in Italy. In less than twelve months, I will be visiting those relatives.

I keep asking myself, "What do I need to do for myself and my family to get the most out of this trip?"

Communicate. I need to be able to communicate with my relatives there. I need to learn Italian, fast. But how?

I have had success learning Spanish in the recent past, and I have a good plan I could follow. Again, I need to commit to it.

I am committed to learning the language that my great-grandparents spoke when they stepped foot in the United States over 100 years ago, no matter what it takes. I know this is yet another way that I can fully embrace my Italian American experience.

Sitting at my kitchen table — Bergen County, NJ
Fall 2015

Getting The Most Out Of Your Journey

For weeks after I had connected with my relatives online, I ignored the thoughts that kept popping up in my head that said to myself, "You need to learn Italian."

Finally, after a Facebook messaging session with my Italian relatives, I realized I could ignore those thoughts no longer; I needed to learn this language before we arrived in Italy. I was picturing my family of five sitting around the dinner table with our Italian relatives—and not being able to speak a word to them. What good would that do?

I had about 10 months before our plane took off—and I had to learn Italian before it did.

The following is the process that I used to become conversational in 10 months. It's not as structured as a language teacher might recommend, but it worked—and honestly, it was a lot of fun.

Start with a Vision

Since we created The Italian American Podcast, I have spent hours researching history—especially immigration patterns and stories. From the book *Immigration* by Dennis Wepman, I learned that approximately 86 percent of Italian immigrants came from southern Italy and Sicily.

This is important to discuss because most of these immigrants who came from the south did not speak traditional Italian—they spoke a dialect local to their region, or even to their village.

If you are planning to learn Italian so that you can communicate during a trip to Italy or in conversations with your relatives, or even if you are familiar with a regional-specific dialect, do yourself a favor and **learn traditional Italian**. Dialects are slowly fading away these days. Kids in Italy are mostly learning traditional Italian, and for that reason, the use of dialects is waning.

On top of that, trying to learn a dialect without actually living in the location where it is spoken is virtually impossible. Even if you did learn it, it might not be helpful if you were to travel to other parts of Italy, especially the north, where many major tourist cities are located.

Before you start learning Italian, you must have a vision for what you want to accomplish. Are you looking to learn the basic words and become conversational, or are you looking to learn from A-to-Z and understand the grammar of the Italian language?

If you have time, the latter is ideal. However, if you, like I did, have limited time to learn, you'll want to shoot for becoming conversational in traditional Italian as quickly as possible. Knowing this from the outset can help you to create your learning plan.

If you have time to learn grammar, then I highly recommend you hire a tutor or enroll in an Italian course.

Many adult community schools have good Italian courses. In fact, I took one—but not until after my trip. My vision for learning was simple: learn to speak to people in Italian as quickly as possible.

This vision helped me to create a learning plan that consisted of the following steps:

- Learn the alphabet and how to pronounce all of the letters and letter combinations.
- Sing as much Italian as I could to practice the pronunciation and get used to making these new sounds.
- Read a book on how to learn Italian with a grammar-based approach; I didn't get deep into grammar but I wanted to have some knowledge.
- Listen to a free podcast to help me learn common words and phrases.
- Hire an online Italian teacher for weekly sessions.
- Engage in Italian conversation as much as possible.

The rest of this chapter discusses these steps in detail, followed by a list of all of the resources I used. It is my intention for you to be able to do this faster than I did by following this plan and using the resources offered (if they feel right for you).

Depending on how much Italian you already know, you may not need to follow these steps exactly. You can pick and choose what suits you.

Learn the Alphabet Again

When you learn a language, you are most likely starting from scratch. In my case, I had spent the previous year learning Spanish for work. Yet, as similar as Spanish and Italian are to one another, I still needed to start from the beginning with Italian because ultimately it is a whole different language.

I wanted to start by learning the alphabet and making sure I could pronounce the letters and the common letter combinations. I found that the best way to do this was to go to my local library and take out children's books on learning Italian. The children's books were very easy for me to follow, and frankly, since I was starting from scratch, I essentially was a child.

This worked perfectly. Not only was it helpful for me, but I would leave the books around the house so that my three children (aged four, seven, and ten) could look through them and start to learn as well.

In addition to the books, I would borrow Italian learning DVDs from the library and play them over and over in the house. Again, I would get DVDs for children since I was starting from the ultimate beginner's level—these were also a big hit with my children.

I can tell you from my experience that learning the alphabet and the sounds was relatively easy, but here are a few of the key letters and combinations that you should master to make your Italian learning process much easier.

- Learn how to announce the Italian vowel sounds very well. The three important ones are "a" (pronounced "ah"), "e" (pronounced "ay"), and, the toughest one for me, "i" (which is pronounced with a double e sound, "ee") Here is a perfect example that encompasses all three of these sounds: the Italian word *grazie* means "thank you," and is pronounced, "grah-zee-ay." Most Americans pronounce it "graz-ee," leaving off the e or "ay" sound at the end.
- The letters "ch" together form the sound of a "k" in Italian, so "che bella," is pronounced, "kay bella," which means, "how beautiful," or more literally, "what beautiful." Most English speakers will pronounce this with the English sound "ch," like in chicken.
- The letter "c," when followed by an "i" or an "e," makes the sound "ch." For example, the most commonly used Italian word, "ciao" (which can be used both for "hello" and "goodbye") is pronounced "chow."

Just being able to tackle these simple challenges will drastically improve your Italian pronunciation.

Use Song to Make Learning Fun

While learning Spanish a few years ago, I met a young entrepreneur who told me about a program he had created to help people learn languages. I initially thought it would be just another language website, but this was different. His philosophy was to teach people the flow of the language, meaning the sounds and pronunciation, before teaching the meaning of the words.

What he would do was select a song in the desired language, provide a detailed breakdown of the pronunciation of the different components of the song, and walk students through singing the song using the correct pronunciation.

His method is called The Mimic Method (MimicMethod.com) and it works because the hardest part of learning languages like Spanish and Italian is the fast pace.

I have taken Spanish for years, and I knew grammar and vocabulary, but as soon as a native speaker started talking to me, I was completely lost. It was too fast for me to understand. After following this method, I could pick up words in conversations and when watching Spanish television programs. And the best part was that singing songs is a fun way to learn!

When it came time to learn Italian, I was saddened to find that there was no Mimic Method course for Italian, so

I had to do it myself. However, it worked almost as well. I selected a few songs in Italian that I thought encompassed a wide range of sounds and sang them repeatedly.

The nice thing about this method is that you can practice it anywhere, at anytime. So if you drive to work everyday, you can simply play the song on your radio repeatedly and sing it out loud, practicing your Italian pronunciation.

I recommend spending your first few weeks or even months doing only this, and then once you become more comfortable with pronunciation and the flow of the language, you can add different kinds of learning activities to your efforts. Regardless of your progress, I recommend that you always continue to sing Italian throughout your entire learning process. Not only is it a fun way to practice pronunciation and increase the rate of your learning, but your family will also be exposed to the sounds—maybe even eventually singing along and learning as well.

You can see a video of me singing in Italian here: http://italianamericanexperience.com/sing.

Learn Consistently Through Different Formats

Before I start to discuss different learning formats, I want to say something that is important to not only language learning or Italian family research but all of life.

In order to become skilled at anything you will need to work on that skill consistently. Whether it is daily, weekly, or whatever schedule works for you, your actions must be consistent. If they are not, you will not become proficient.

As your pronunciation improves, I recommend that you start to utilize some different formats to continue learning, including both audio and visual. In my case, I found a free podcast called Coffee Break Italian and a wonderful book entitled *Living Italian: A Grammar-Based Course* (which came with a CD).

The podcast offered short, ten-minute episodes on different Italian topics, focused mostly on grammar, but also featured some conversations. It allowed me to listen to Italian interactions and try to decipher them.

The book, *Living Italian*, was strictly focused on grammar; it offered simple exercises with an answer key and explanations to ensure I was learning and understanding the language beyond just its sounds.

When it came to the practical use of Italian, I think the podcast may have been the most helpful resource, because it gave real-life examples that I remembered when I was in Italy. For example, in one episode they would walk you through how to order train tickets in Italian and then have you listen to sample conversations around this topic. I still listen to the podcast to this day.

With regards to consistency, I recommend engaging in these learning methods at the same time every day so that they become habitual. For me, I would listen to the podcast in the morning for about 10 minutes while driving the kids to school, and then every night I would sit on the couch, with a cup of tea, and read the book for 20 minutes.

In total, I spent 25 to 30 minutes per day studying. That may not sound like a lot when you are learning a language, but the time adds up quickly; if you stick with this pace for a year, you'll have put in close to 200 hours of studying.

You will have much more success learning with this approach than you would by only taking a class once a week without much additional study in between lessons.

Create Accountable Conversations

The absolute best way to learn any language is through conversation—either by simply listening to conversations or actively engaging in them. The problem with this is you are most likely learning the language outside of its origin country, so you may have no one to converse with—but there are easy ways to solve this issue.

For example, I found a wonderful language learning website named iTalki (italki.com). This website allows you to create a profile and list both your native language and the language you are learning. It then allows people with the opposite language profile to find you, connect with you, and converse with you.

Let's say I create a profile, designate my native language as English, and the language I am learning as Italian. Within days, native-speaking Italians who want to learn English will most likely contact me. Then, if I am comfortable with any or all of these individuals, I can arrange to speak with them through Skype. If you are not aware of Skype, it is an application that allows you to make video calls to people around the world for free.

These exchanges are invaluable to your quest to learn a new language. By having these conversations on video calls, you can see the person as you communicate; this makes conversation much easier than trying to converse only over the phone. You can also watch them mouth the words—which makes for a better learning experience.

Again, I have to talk about consistency here. This is all great, but who is going to hold you accountable and motivate you to have these conversations on a regular basis? No one—besides yourself. Unfortunately, I have found that if we rely solely on ourselves, no matter how motivated we may be, the stress of everyday life may overcome us.

To that end, iTalki also allows you to hire verified instructors through their website, instead of only having conversations with Italian speakers. This means you can have a teacher in Italy actually teaching you the language, in a one-on-one relationship, and at a relatively affordable price. I hired an instructor for $18 per 30-minute session for a total of 20 sessions.

This adds accountability into your learning process in several ways. First of all, any time you pay for something, there is an inherent drive not to waste your money. Second, you have to purchase lessons in packages, which requires you to have multiple lessons with the same instructor. Lastly, the credits expire at some point, which pushes you to meet your instructor on a regular basis to use up the credits you paid for.

I hired an Italian teacher in Rome and he was wonderful. He wasn't easy, either—he was strict, which made me even more focused on doing my assignments correctly in between the weekly sessions. His teaching style was very conversation-based. For homework each week he would give me audio files containing conversations that I would have to listen to and type out. He swore this was the best way to learn Italian and ensure that his students could engage in conversations when in Italy—and he was right.

More important than all of the learning actions discussed in this chapter, you must be confident in yourself and understand that speaking a new language is not a skill we are born with. However, it *is* something that anyone can learn to do with consistent learning and practice.

The difference between knowing and not knowing Italian will have a dramatic impact on the enjoyment level of your trip(s) to Italy. Trust me, I know from experience—as you will read about in the next section of this book.

ACTION ITEMS FOR YOU:
Language Learning Tools

The following is a summary of the language learning steps mentioned in this chapter, along with associated resources. (Regarding resources, please note there are many different ones available for learning the Italian language online at different price points—the following are merely the tools I used.)

1. Start with a Vision

This step requires only some thought and a blank piece of paper. Set goals for what level of Italian you want to progress to by the time of your trip. This will not only be affected by the amount of time you have until your trip—but also be by your budget. For example, if you have a sizeable budget, then you can work with a language teacher on a weekly basis—or perhaps even more often.

2. Learn the Alphabet Again

Start simple. I recommend starting the process by learning the alphabet, as well as the pronunciation of key letter combinations. I don't have specific books for this step, but I recommend you start by visiting your public library and taking out children's books and DVDs on learning Italian.

3. Use Song to Make Learning Fun

Before getting into vocabulary, sing songs in Italian that will allow you to get used to pronouncing these new sounds. Not only will this be fun, but it will also make conversations easy when the time comes, as it will help you get used to the pace of the Italian language. I sang Bocelli's Time to Say Goodbye over and over.

4. Learn Consistently Through Different Formats

To learn a new language, you must work on that language every day. Doing so through various formats will make it easier. For example, I mentioned that I listened to a free podcast and also read a book on Italian Grammar. [Resources: *Coffee Break Italian Podcast* at RadioLingua.com, and the book *Living Italian: A Grammar-Based Course* by Maria Valgimigli & Derek Aust]

5. Create Accountable Conversations

You must converse in Italian as often as possible to become conversational. Obviously spending time in Italy is the best way to do this, however I was able to find instructors and native Italian speakers to engage with over Skype prior to my trip abroad. You should also consider local community schools that often offer affordable, small-group Italian classes. [Resource: italki.com]

In addition to those indicated above, here are some other language learning resources:
- fluentin3months.com (website)
- duolingo.com (website)
- rocketlanguages.com (website)
- *Italian Now! Level 1: L'italiano d'oggi!* by Marcel Danesi, Ph.D. (book)

You can download a list of these steps and websites, and find other helpful resources, at FortyDaysInItaly.com.

Remember, speaking a new language is not a skill you are born with—but anyone can learn languages with some consistent hard work and determination.

Chapter 5

Planning the Trip of a Lifetime to Italy

Where do I start? I have never planned a trip of this magnitude. Forty days in Italy with three young children.

Where do we go? What sites do we visit?

I have to remember that the main focus of this trip is family. I want to plan the trip in a way that ensures we can spend time and connect with our Italian relatives. I also want to build in downtime for my family along the way so we don't get worn out.

I am just going to take this planning process one step at a time.

Sitting at my desk — Bergen County, NJ
Winter 2015–2016

Create a Vision for Your Trip

Now it's time to dive into planning the ultimate trip to Italy. In my opinion, the ultimate trip to Italy is one where you connect with your heritage, whether by visiting relatives, or, if there are no living relatives that you know of, visiting the ancestral villages where your ancestors immigrated from. That is my vision—you have to figure out what yours is.

It is important to have a vision for your trip to Italy before you start the planning process because your vision should drive all of the planning decisions that you make.

The biggest question to consider should be what the purpose is of the trip. Are you visiting Italy to go to the major cities and do sightseeing? Are you planning to visit Italy to visit your ancestors' villages and learn about your heritage? Are you planning to do both?

While there are no wrong answers, the answers can hugely impact the makeup of your trip—including the length and the cost. Most Italian-Americans' ancestors immigrated to the U.S. from southern Italy and Sicily. While getting to these locations may be more costly than traveling to a major city, staying in these locations might be cheaper—and you may be able to make your money last longer in small remote villages.

My trip was a combination of both. My original reason for visiting Italy was to celebrate my Uncle Carl's

60th birthday. He is American but decided to rent a villa in Sicily for the occasion and invite our entire family.

In this chapter, I will walk you through the planning process that my wife and I used for our 40-day trip. Remember, we are not travel agents, nor are we experienced travelers of Italy—which is important because my guess is that you probably aren't, either! My hope is that you can learn from our mistakes as well as our successes and plan your own trip of a lifetime.

Selecting the Time of Year

Once you have decided to travel to Italy and you have a good handle on the vision for your trip, the next step is to decide what time of the year you plan to travel. For my wife and I the decision was easy; we planned to take our young children with us, so we knew we would be going in the summer when they were off from school. You may have more options than we did.

Again, you have to consider the reasons you are going on the trip. If you are going to mostly do sightseeing and you have flexibility, you should consider going during off-peak times, which will be cheaper and less crowded.

In travel-industry jargon, the year is divided into three seasons: peak season (roughly mid-June through August), shoulder season (April through mid-June and September through October), and off-season (November through

March). Also keep in mind the weather, as it can get extremely hot in Italy during the summer.

If you are traveling mainly to visit family or your ancestral villages, the time of year might not be as important—unless your family depends on a particular livelihood, in which case their work schedule might be something to plan around. For example, my family in both the Napoli region and Sicily make olive oil. Therefore, if I ever want to make the oil with them (and I plan to), I will need to visit them in the fall during an oil-making year, as they only make the oil every other year.

There are plenty of travel planning websites that can help you nail down the best time of the year to go. Think seriously about what you want to accomplish during the trip and then select the time of year that will best facilitate you accomplishing that goal.

Deciding on the Length of Your Trip

When planning a trip overseas, the length of the trip is critically important. In my opinion, if you really want to understand and learn about your destination, you need to spend time there. You need to give yourself time to talk to locals and get to know how and why they live the way they do.

Spending extended periods of time away from home may not be easy to arrange; however, with the increase in people utilizing the Internet to work remotely, it has become simpler and more common.

It is for this reason that my wife and I, both 38 years old at the time of our summer trip, were able to stay in Italy for 40 days with our children. At the time, my wife had a job that was scheduled around the school year, so she had summers off. As far as my employment goes, it's not your typical job. I am an entrepreneur and I spend most of my time writing and developing content that helps people. I write books and articles, record podcasts, and shoot videos that are all focused on helping people in specific niches.

My recommendation to you is that if you plan to visit Italy, especially if it is to learn about your heritage, try and stay as long as you can. I would recommend at least 17 days. Also, consider remaining in one place as long as possible. A common mentality among travelers is to attempt to visit as many towns and cities as they can in their allotted travel time. The benefit of this mentality is you get to see a lot of things—but the downside is that the lack depth of the experience in each location can make the experiences less moving.

We made some last-minute adjustments to our itinerary that cut out a few stops and lengthened our stays in the remaining locations. Even with those changes, if I had to do it again, I would have visited fewer places.

To give you a point of reference, this is how our trip was laid out:

- Lerici (including visits to Pisa and Le Cinque Terre)
- Rome (including a full day in the Vatican)
- Sorrento (including trips to Pompeii and Capri)
- Paestum (including trips to Sarno and Albanella—our ancestral villages)
- Agrigento (including trips to Catania and Enna)
- Trecastagni (including day trip to Mount Etna)
- Sortino (including day trip to Noto)
- Napoli and Avella

We averaged roughly five days in each location, but there were some I wish we could have spent still more time in. The longer you stay in a location, the more you can learn and enjoy, and the better you can connect with the local citizens. Either way, as an absolute minimum, I would recommend four days and three nights in each place.

The length of your trip is an important component—but one which many times is dictated by various constraints that are out of your control. If you have a good vision, you should try to select the length and locations to visit that will allow you to best achieve it.

Regions to Visit in Italy

Obviously, a critical part of your Italy trip planning is deciding where to go.

While I may sound like a broken record, you must rely on your vision for your trip to make these decisions, as it will make them so much easier. If your trip will mainly be focused on family history research, then you will most likely plan to visit the regions of Italy where your ancestors' origin villages are located.

You may decide that your first trip to Italy will be focused on more touristic activities in the major cities like Rome, Florence, and Venice. That is completely up to you—but if at all possible, I would recommend that you do make sure to visit some of these major cities and tourist attractions. In an ideal situation, you might be able to do an extended trip where you can spend a week to 10 days sightseeing and the rest of the trip in your ancestral villages.

For reference, my ancestors came from the following locations in Italy:

- Giuseppe Baselice (maternal great-grandfather) — Sarno, Italy (Campania)
- Maria Paciullo (maternal great-grandmother) — Sarno, Italy (Campania)
- Carlo Piraneo (maternal great-grandfather) — Sortino, Italy (Sicilia)

- Rosina Blancato (maternal great-grandmother) — Sortino, Italy (Sicilia)
- Germano Salese (paternal great grandfather) — Albanella, Italy (Campania)
- Anna Falcone (paternal great-grandmother) — Unknown
- Antonio Fasano (paternal great-grandfather) — Controne, Italy (Campania)
- Antoinette Carillo (paternal great-grandmother) — Serre, Italy (Campania)*

While writing this section of the book, I discovered that Great-Grandma Antoinette was born in Serre. I went back through all of the documentation in her profile in my online family tree and the information was in her naturalization record. The village name was small and smudged on the document, but with some quick Google searches, I was able to figure out that it was Serre.

I show you where my ancestors are from so you can get a sense of what we were thinking when we selected the regions to visit. Remember, we had 40 days in Italy, so we had a a lot of time to work with.

We decided to start out in the north and spend the first week on the beaches of Lerici so the kids could get acclimated to the time difference. It was a difficult location to get to from New Jersey, but once there, it offered some amazing day trips (which I will detail later). Our time up north also allowed us to visit the eternal city of Rome, a place we really wanted the kids to see.

We then headed south to spend some time in Sorrento, where we were able to visit Capri and Pompeii—both excellent trips. Then, in mid July, we headed to the areas where our family lived and spent most of the rest of the trip with them.

It was good variety, but there are definitely some things we'll do different next time. Part II of this book will detail our trip, but for now, stay focused on selecting the regions you want to visit in Italy as this is a major part of your trip planning.

Getting to and from Italy

Your trips to and from Italy are very important parts of the trip when it comes to budgeting both time and money. There are so many ways that you can save money on this element—and one of the biggest ones is accumulating travel points through credit card purchases.

I don't think it would have been possible for my wife and I to take this trip with our kids if we hadn't spent 10 years building up enough credit card points to pay for all five of our round trip plane tickets to Italy. That alone saved us over five thousand dollars and, quite frankly, was one of the key factors that made this trip go from a dream to a reality.

Here are some things you should consider when booking your flights to and from Italy.

- Sign up for a credit card that gives you travel points or miles for every dollar spent. This is especially important if you plan to travel to Italy or elsewhere on a regular basis. We have used a Chase United card, but Capital One also has a good card that allows you to use your points on any travel expenses. Once you have the credit card, use it to pay for everything (as long as you are also responsible enough to also pay it off regularly). We were lucky enough to be able to use it on my children's daycare for years, but we do use it on everything—even to pay our cable bills.

- Consider traveling during the off-peak season if it fits your schedule and vision. Traveling at off-peak times can greatly reduce the cost of airline tickets.

- Utilize non-popular airlines if they make sense to your plans. There are several smaller airline companies that offer very affordable flights to Italy. In fact, there is one airline that flies direct to Sicily from JFK in New York City. Remember when I said to make your plans thinking about not only money, but also about your time? Eliminating a stopover could gain you almost a full extra day on your trip—which means a lot when you have limited time to travel.

- Try to minimize modes of transportation needed. This should be done when planning the locations you want to visit. For example, our initial trip to Lerici required a shuttle to the airport, two plane rides, two train rides, and a taxi—all with three children under 10 years old. We won't be doing that again. Not only can multiple legs of a trip be stressful, but they also add a lot of time and cost to your trip. If we do it again, we will probably stay in a city near the airport for the first leg of the trip.

- Look into airlines and airports that are kid friendly if you are traveling with young children. One of our stops on the way to Italy was at Zurich airport, where there was an amazing family lounge with activities for the kids and a bed where my wife slept. As with many things we saw and places we visited over the 40 days, we look back at that family lounge as an important place where we were all able to recharge in the midst of an unbearable 24 hours of travel.

- Understand the baggage rules on your plane. Know exactly what is permitted and what costs extra, especially if you are on a tight budget; two oversized bags can easily cost you more than $100 per flight.

Many of these things we didn't know (and therefore, didn't do) during our trip; one of the primary reasons I am writing this book is so that you will know what we didn't—and have a much easier time as a result.

Transportation Within Italy

Once you've made it *to* Italy, another potential big expense is transportation *within* Italy. Believe it or not, this ended up being our biggest expense—mainly because the rental cars were extremely expensive.

I would try to avoid rental cars as much as possible next time, although in some parts of southern Italy and Sicily you do need them—especially if you want to travel to remote areas or take day trips away from the place you are staying.

Here are some things to consider when planning your method of transportation within Italy:

- Firstly, look at your itinerary and decide where and when you will need a rental car—or if you will need one at all. Like I said, if you are spending multiple days and weeks in remote areas of Italy, a rental car will give you the valuable freedom and flexibility to travel where you want, when you want.
- Should you plan to rent a car, rent manual over automatic. If you don't know how to drive a manual shift, consider learning. I am not kidding. For one of the legs of our trip, which was about

two weeks long, it cost $700 more to rent an automatic shift car.

- If you plan to drive at all in Italy, consider obtaining an international driving license through AAA. You can find information on this here: https://www.aaa.com/vacation/idpf.html
- Contact your auto insurance company and find out what insurance you should take out when renting a car in Italy. Your U.S. auto insurance may or may **not** cover you.
- Consider taking the damage insurance policy on a rental car. Drivers in Italy can be crazy, so you will want to make sure that you are covered. My father's rental car was hit several times in Italy, but thankfully he had the needed coverage.
- Book your rental car(s) in advance of your trip. In one location, I had accidentally booked a larger-than-needed car—but there were no options to change it because they were sold out. This is especially important if you go during peak travel season.
- Consider using trains to travel from major city to major city. Most of the trains in Italy were clean, efficient, and not too expensive. In fact, if you purchase tickets ahead of time through Eurail or Trenitalia, young children ride for free. Here are the websites: http://www.trainitaly.us and http://www.eurail.com/eurail-passes.

- When booking train tickets, consider going First Class if you can afford it. In some cases, since the children were free in either class, it only cost us $40 or $50 more in total for us to purchase First Class tickets. The additional cost was worth it as we had better air conditioning and more space. This proved to be invaluable in Italy in the summer—especially on a three-hour train ride with three young children.

- When planning your trip, consider using taxis as opposed to multiple modes of public transportation. When we got off the train in Napoli, we had pre-booked a ferry ride to Sorrento. So we had to take a taxi from the Napoli train station to the ferry port, a ferry to the Sorrento port, and a taxi to our apartment in Sorrento. It cost us a little over $100, but more than that, it cost us over two hours. There was a cab driver waiting on the train platform who said he would have taken us right to our apartment in Sorrento for $100.

- If you plan to hire a driver, especially if you plan to do so in or around small Italian villages, consider doing so **before** you leave the U.S.— especially if your Italian language is limited. You can do this by contacting a tour company local to that region or a local travel agent. This is especially important if you plan to take a day trip to your ancestral origin villages. These trips may be lengthy and costly. By reserving a driver beforehand, you can ensure that you will have transportation while also being able to evaluate and nail down your cost.

Staying in Italy on a Budget

The general perception Americans hold of travel in Italy is that it is very expensive. That is not necessarily the case if you commit to traveling on a budget. In our case, we are by no means wealthy. We were also traveling with three young children, so in order for all five of us to be able to afford 40 days in Italy, we had to be extremely frugal.

As a point of reference, I want to share with you the cost of our trip. For 40 days in Italy, for our family of five, it cost approximately $11,000 out of pocket. I say "out of pocket" because we rented out our home in New Jersey—the $11,000 amount is after I credited our cost with the rental income.

If you examine that number more, it didn't even really feel like $11,000—it felt like much less. If we were home, we would still have had regular food and living costs and we most likely would have sent the kids to summer camps. We also would have taken our usual weeklong vacation at the Jersey Shore. Therefore, our real expense was probably closer to $5,000 or $6,000.

Keep in mind that credit card reward points covered our flights to and from Italy. This went a long way towards keeping our costs down. Also, know that of the 40 days in Italy, we stayed nine nights with relatives at no cost to us.

Here are some strategies we used to keep costs down. Your budget and vision for your trip may be different than ours, so traveling on a budget might not be as important. Either way, you may find some of these helpful.

- Instead of staying in hotels, we rented apartments through two websites: AirBnB (airbnb.com) and Booking.com. This provided huge savings compared to the costs of traditional hotels. In some areas, we were able to stay in an apartment that slept all five of us comfortably for under $100 per night.

- We stayed mostly within the center of the cities we visited to avoid added transportation costs when we wanted to do sightseeing. Consider the location of your hotels or apartments with respect to the sights you plan to visit.

- We ate out at restaurants rarely. If you have children or if you plan to travel for an extended period of time, consider shopping at supermarkets and cooking your meals (also why apartments are important). Over 40 days, we probably ate dinner out fifteen times or less—and most of those were when our Italian family members took us out. The five of us only went to restaurants as a family once per each city that we stayed; that was our own rule. You can get amazing produce for very low cost at both supermarkets and outdoor markets in most Italian cities.

- We regularly snacked on apples, carrots, and almonds while walking around during the day. Of course, we also brought water bottles for everyone, which is important for general health but also to avoid dehydration in the Italian heat. When taking day trips, pack water and snacks. This tip may seem insignificant, but it can save you a lot of money. In some tourist areas of Italy, sitting down for a snack and a drink can cost a ridiculous amount of money.

Food can be a huge source of expense in Italy. Now, of course, one of the main reasons for visiting Italy is to experience the food, no doubt about that. However, if you are traveling for an extended period of time, then depending on the location, restaurants can start to get very expensive. Some of the best mozzarella di bufala (mozzarella from the milk of buffalo) that we ate was purchased at the deli counter in a supermarket.

If you are traveling without children and you are in remote areas of Italy, you can eat out very inexpensively on a regular basis. You will find small family-run restaurants in most small villages where there is no menu, but there are large, fresh, delicious, authentic Italian meals.

When You Should Splurge in Italy

As you know by now, we were traveling through Italy on a tight budget and with three young children. But when you take a rare trip, especially back to the home of your ancestors, there are some things that I recommend you do regardless of how much they cost.

While my wife and I were extremely frugal and very aware of our daily spending on the trip, here are a few items that I would say are worth spending money on—even if it's a little beyond your budget.

- **Educational Resources**
  We took several tours while in Italy, including a wonderful tour of the Vatican, as well as a tour of Pompeii (the small Italian village well-known for the catastrophic eruption of Mount Vesuvius in 79 A.D.). These were tours that I researched and booked ahead of the trip, but there are also plenty of tours you can find while in Italy. I believe that learning the history of places that you visit adds a wonderful dimension to your travel experience and you should make every effort to find tours or other educational resources, like books, to enrich your trip.

- **Special Excursions**
  There will most likely be opportunities to take various day trips or excursions from the primary locations you are staying in Italy. In many cases, while these may be expensive, they can

provide experiences and memories that will last a lifetime. While in Pompeii, we never visited Mount Vesuvius, and my wife was upset about it for a week or two afterwards. However, we were able to make up for it by taking the kids to the top of Mount Etna in Sicily. Not a cheap endeavor, but one I will always remember. Another excursion that was well worth it was a day trip to the beautiful island of Capri. Again, not cheap, but probably the most beautiful beach I have been on—ever. These excursions can provide memories, photos, and videos that well outweigh the costs.

- **First-Class Travel Accommodations**
  As I mentioned earlier, in some scenarios, it makes sense to pay extra for first class. For example, an extra $50 or so gave our family of five our own air-conditioned compartment on the train. With three kids, believe me, this is worth a lot more than $50.

- **Safety**
  Another item not to be sacrificed for the sake of your budget is safety. If you are deciding whether to hop on a bus late at night in an unfamiliar part of town or pay an extra $20 to take a taxi, take the taxi every time. It's just not worth the risk.

- **Family**
  There were a few times during our 40 days in Italy that we added expenses to the trip to make

extra visits to our family or an ancestral village of one of my relatives. At the time, it felt like a lot of money to rent a car for a few more days than we had originally planned. However, looking back at the photos of those extra days spent with family in the mountains, I would have paid double. Don't sacrifice time with your family or in special places in Italy for a few hundred dollars—you'll regret it every time.

- **Food**
  The only time I would recommend splurging on food in Italy is if you are in a major city and there is a food specific to the region that you must have. Otherwise, you can find amazing, relatively inexpensive food throughout the country. Whether at a small family-owned restaurant or fresh produce market, we ate very well (and inexpensively) for 40 days with ease.

As you can tell, most of these tips revolve around trading money for memories—which is always a worthwhile deal.

ACTION ITEMS FOR YOU:
Travel Planning Tips

In this chapter I focused on travel planning—a critical component of maximizing your time while in Italy. The following is a summary of some of the key actions I recommended you take in planning your next trip to Italy—or anywhere for that matter:

1. Cast a Vision for the Trip

Create a clear vision of what you hope to take away from your trip. Is your goal to see many historical sites? Visit your ancestors' birthplaces? Or maybe both?

2. Timing Matters

Select times of the year that will best help you to achieve your vision for your trip based on any scheduling limitations you have. I recommend traveling during off-peak seasons if possible; your trip will cost less and there will be fewer crowds.

3. Length of Stay

Select a length for your trip that will also allow you to achieve your vision. Again, you may have limitations due to work or other responsibilities, but I recommend trying to stay for at least two to two-and-a-half weeks.

4. Location, Location, Location

Decide on the regions of Italy you want to visit, again based on your vision for your trip. If your time and budget permit, consider spending one portion of the trip sightseeing and the other portion visiting family or ancestral villages. If you are lucky, maybe you can do both in the same region of Italy.

5. Save Money with Travel Rewards

Use travel rewards to save money on transportation to and from Italy. There are many good credit card rewards programs available and air travel rewards are a great way to save a substantial amount of money.

6. Getting Around

Travel wisely within Italy; use trains as often as possible as rental cars and car services can be expensive. That being said, if you prefer to travel by car, attempt to book drivers and rentals in advance of your trip. When renting a car, opt for manual transmission if possible to save money.

7. Saving on Room and Board

Consider saving money by renting apartments through websites like AirBnB and Booking.com instead of using hotels—especially if you are traveling with children or other relatives. Also consider shopping at supermarkets and cooking in your apartment to save even more money.

8. When to Spend

Spend on items that are truly important to you and your family, like tours and other educational resources, excursions, travel upgrades (where it makes sense), and, of course, safety.

I know that this gives you a lot of things to consider, but by implementing a few of these items, you can save thousands of dollars—and possibly stay in Italy longer You can download a list of these action items, and find other helpful resources, a FortyDaysInItaly.com.

Alright, that's enough of planning; it's time for us to travel to Italy together.

PART II:
The Trip of a Lifetime

Chapter 6

Italy — Arrival & Acclimation

We have made it. We overcame all of the doubts caused by people telling us "You can't travel to Italy with three young children. You can't spend an extended amount of time overseas with kids and still do your work."

As usual, I woke up early; the rest of my family is asleep, since we arrived at our apartment here in our first stop in Italy (Lerici), late last night.

I got dressed, quietly closed the creaking front door of the small one-bedroom apartment, and walked out into the Italian morning air.

A few minutes later, I find myself standing in the main square of Lerici, looking out at the water shining in the strong sun. It is definitely a moment to remember. While I have been in northern Italy for less than 24 hours, and am still far from my living relatives, in many ways it feels like I am home. I have come a long way from sitting at Grandma's kitchen table two years ago.

Standing in the main square in Lerici, Italy
July 2016

Time Travel

Our physical trip to Italy from New Jersey with our three children was a nightmare in many ways; I have no intentions of sugar-coating it. Piling our luggage into a shuttle close to home. Waiting in lines in the airport to board our first plane. Spending nine hours on a flight to Zurich, during which our kids just wouldn't go to sleep because they were so excited. A long layover in Zurich, which we only made it through thanks to a wonderful family lounge. A cramped taxi ride to the train station in Florence after getting off of the second plane.

We had the disastrous experience at the train station I mentioned earlier where we almost missed our train to Pisa. Then, a broken elevator in the Pisa train station almost caused us to miss our connecting train to Spezia. On our final taxi ride to Lerici, I almost passed out in the back seat due to heat exhaustion. But nevertheless, we made it to our first stop: Lerici, Italy.

My wife and I agreed that the next lengthy trip would be comprised of only one or two transition points—as opposed to five. We also agreed that next time we would go to a major city that was easy to access from the airport first; I urge you to consider the same.

Lerici is about an hour-and-a-half drive northwest of Florence, and an hour-and-a-half drive southeast of Genoa. It is located in the region of Italy known as

Liguria, also known as the Italian Riviera. This region is famous for being the origin location of pesto.

We chose Lerici as our first stop for a few reasons. One, we had read that young children could need up to a week to adjust to the time difference, so we figured Lerici offered many beaches where they could lazily get acclimated. We also wanted to take the kids to Pisa to see the leaning tower and Le Cinque Terre, which were both easily accessible from Lerici.

The trip to Italy was a trying experience (and not the smoothest start to our adventure) but it was also a very emotional trip for me. I couldn't help but feel like I was traveling back in time. Some people refer to these trips where you are seeking information about your ancestors as "voyages of discovery." I think that is a great way to refer to them; as you will see in the coming pages, it really can be one discovery after the next.

For me, it felt like I had come full circle. My great-grandparents, poor and looking for a better life for their families, came to the United States in the early 20th century. Here I was, more than one hundred years later, bringing my family back to the homeland to learn about where they came from.

The First Meal

Arriving in Lerici, after the rough twenty-four hours of travel, we had just enough energy to lug our bags up the narrow alleyway to our apartment and a quick tour from the owner. As soon as she left, all of our stomachs growled at the same time. We were ready for our first meal in Italy.

Our first meal together in Italy after a brutal 24 hours of travel.

We strolled down the alleyway together. I am not sure how I remember this happening, as I was completely delirious. I was happy that we made it, yes, but running on fumes at best. We sat down at one of the many outdoor restaurants in the main square of Lerici.

We found a nice place; honestly, the pesto was average—but this meal wasn't about the food. It was a celebration of a long journey that was over two years in the making. While we were all exhausted, there was an aura of success and excitement at the table. They could have served us cardboard and everyone would have been smiling. We had made it.

As I waited for the bill, my wife took the kids back to the apartment. The waiter brought me a small bottle of Limoncello, a shot glass, and the bill. I sat there for about five minutes, sipping the Limoncello, and watching the sunset over the Gulf of La Spezia. I couldn't help but think to myself, "This is going to be fun."

Acclimating to Italia

Lerici is truly a beautiful place. The sun gleams upon the gulf for most of the day, and it is especially beautiful early in the morning and at night. It is a vacation destination for Italians, kind of like the Jersey Shore of northern Italy—except it's the Italian Riviera. This was great for many reasons—one of them being I was able to practice a lot of Italian (as there were no Americans in Lerici).

I enjoyed the sunrise with an espresso, then went to the local market and shopped. As I mentioned earlier, we spent most of our time cooking all of our meals in our apartments to stay on a budget. The supermarkets in Italy are so different than the ones in the U.S. The produce is unbelievably fresh and plentiful, and you can find all different kinds of meat and fish depending on where you are in Italy.

I was trying to immerse myself in the culture right from the beginning. I was more confident with my Italian than I thought I'd be, and the Italian people were incredibly friendly, making me feel comfortable speaking their language.

I got back to the apartment to find my wife up but our three kids still out cold. "I wish they slept this late every day," I told my wife, smiling. Eventually, they woke up and we went exploring, spending some time on a little, hidden beach behind the Castello di Lerici (Lerici Castle). Castles, beaches, pesto, gelato… only in Italy.

We were all dragging at first; however, the kids seemed to get a lot of energy late in the evening and we couldn't get them to bed until 11 p.m. It normally wouldn't have bothered us, considering the circumstances, but our plan was to get an early train to Pisa the next morning.

Torre di Pisa

I wish we had also spent our second full day relaxing, but we decided to take the kids to the Leaning Tower of Pisa instead. We woke them up, took a bus from Lerici back to Spezia, and then a train to Pisa. We actually

Italy — Arrival & Acclimation

had a laugh and took a photo next to the elevator at the station that had been broken on our initial trip through a few days earlier.

This is me being a tourist and having some fun in the Piazza dei Miracoli in Pisa.

After a 30-minute walk from the Pisa train station, in the hot sun, there it was. We stared up at the first real recognizable sign that we were in Italy. For the kids, this was a landmark that they recognized from textbooks and images on the computer: the Leaning Tower of Pisa, or in Italian, *Torre di Pisa*.

Seeing the smiles on the kids' faces when they saw the Tower was special. We walked the square and took the customary photos where we pretended to hold the Tower up.

We had a wonderful dinner near the Tower. I had gnocchi in a Gorgonzola sauce, and some vino. Then it was the long walk and trip back to Lerici. At one point, we spent 60 minutes at a bus stop in Spezia—but it was worth it. That image of the Leaning Tower was as good a "Welcome to Italy" sign as we could get.

Le Cinque Terre

If you are an Italian American, you know that there is one thing that we are really not good at doing: relaxing. After a long day of travel, one beach day, and a trip to Pisa, it would make sense to rest, right? No; we were up early the next morning, ready to board a ferry headed to Le Cinque Terre.

Le Cinque Terre, which in English translates as The Five Lands, is a series of very old seaside villages along the Italian Riviera coastline. In each of the five villages, colorful houses and vineyards are set along steep terraces, the harbors are filled with fishing boats, and amazing restaurants and beaches can be found tucked away throughout.

If you don't know Le Cinque Terre by name, you would know it if you saw it—the images of these cliff-side villages are often shown on postcards and in travel magazines. Since there was a ferry directly from Lerici, we felt we had to go.

The views on the boat ride were truly breathtaking. The kids were tired, but boat rides tend to excite kids and keep them interested and engaged. You have the ability to get on and off the ferry at each of the five villages, but with the kids, we thought it best to just get off at the last stop, Monterosso, and spend the day there.

The stone beach was beautiful. The water was clear. A picturesque little town with alleyways full of great restaurants and shops. It was here that we had our first pizza in Italy. I regret this, as the pizza here was no better than that in New York. We should have waited until we headed further south, as later in the trip I would taste pizza like I have never tasted it before.

If you like beaches, boat rides, and small Italian villages, Le Cinque Terre is for you. It does get very busy with tourists in peak season, but we still enjoyed it. There are paths along the coast that you can hike from one village to the next; I hope to do that one day. but that will be a trip for just my wife and me, (or maybe the entire family when the kids get older).

We had already seen some breathtaking sights on our trip in just the first few days. Knowing that my living relatives were hours from me was a great feeling. It almost felt like they were pulling me towards them. Meeting them couldn't come fast enough.

Space for Breathing and Experiencing

I joke about Italian Americans not being able to relax. I think that our work ethic is in our blood from our immigrant ancestors. Through my work hosting The Italian American Podcast, I have confirmed that it's not just my family that can't sit still—it's our Italian American community as a whole.

That being said, an extended trip to Italy, especially in the summer, requires pockets of time dedicated to rest and relaxation. I refer to this time as space for breathing and experiencing. These breaks allow you to really experience the culture and the people as opposed to rushing from one sight to the next. (Oh, and I guess they also allow your mind and body a chance to recuperate, as well.)

We spent the last two days in Lerici on beaches with hundreds of vacationing Italians. The kids snorkeled and built sandcastles. I watched and listened to Italian families gathering from different parts of the country to enjoy vacationing together.

Here's me and Francesco, my new Italian friend.

While I was playing in the water with the kids, I met an Italian man in his fifties named Francesco. He and his wife were originally from the area around Naples but had moved north 15 years ago. His three kids, as well as his grandchildren, were there. We talked in Italian for two hours. This was amazing practice for me and it gave me some much-needed confirmation that once we met my family I would need to speak Italian to really connect with them.

Francesco and I spoke about life and the differences in culture between Italy and the United States. He was a very nice man, with a beautiful family, and we ended the day by taking a wonderful photo together.

Downtime, especially when traveling, can really allow you to immerse yourself in the culture and understand how people live, think, and thrive.

This is why I believe in traveling for an extended period of time whenever possible; it provides the freedom to schedule built-in time meant for relaxing and experiencing things, which results in a much richer experience than constant sightseeing and tours would. This desire to experience the local culture would grow as we got deeper into the trip and closer to my roots.

Lessons Learned from Lerici

Here are some lessons learned from the first leg of our trip in Lerici that you can consider when planning your trip, whether it be a voyage of discovery or a sightseeing excursion.

Minimize the number of transfer points and/or modes of transportation.
Instead of scheduling two train transfers for one trip, try to stay in a location close to your first stop for a while. This is especially important if you are traveling with kids, or if you are unable to make 30-second sprints through terminals. Doing so will reduce stress and keep your energy (and interest) higher during your trip.

When traveling to Italy from the US, give yourself a day to recover from jet lag, if possible.

While it may take more than that (I have heard it can take a few days to adjust for most healthy adults, and up to a week for children.), jumping right into any kind of tour or activity on day one could negatively affect your energy for longer than you'd like. I have heard it can take a few days to adjust for most healthy adults, and up to a week for children.

Do some research into the foods local to the region prior to your trip.

Believe it or not, I didn't realize that pesto originated in Liguria until I picked up a jar of pesto in a supermarket in New Jersey two weeks before our trip. It always makes the trip more special when you can really embrace the local food—and it is usually fantastic.

Plan to visit a mix of famous sites (e.g., the Tower of Pisa) and other not-so-touristy spots, like small local churches or restaurants off the beaten path.

This will give you a varied experience and the best of both the tourist and the local experiences. Plus, the off-the-beaten path locations will likely be less expensive and will help you keep costs reasonable.

Schedule downtime in your trip for experiencing your surroundings and fully immersing yourself in the culture.

You may feel like you don't want to focus on this when planning, but these are the moments you will remember more than the big city sights. Use the language as much as possible and try to feel as if you were at home.

I realize everyone is different, but my hope is that at least one of these recommendations will give you a deeper experience during your trip. You can download a list of these lessons learned, and find other helpful resources, at FortyDaysInItaly.com.

CHAPTER 7

The Eternal City and the Amalfi Coast

Was this trip really a good idea? Is it too late to go home? So far it's been very stressful, what with all of the travel and missed trains and unfamiliar places for the kids.

Is it too late to pack up and go home?

No. It's just a rough start to the trip. My Italian is holding up well, the landscapes are beautiful, and we are only a few hundred miles from our living relatives in Italy.

I am in a place that most Italian Americans would die to be right now. Let's keep moving forward. Good things are coming.

Tempo al tempo (all in good time).

**My internal conversation while waiting for a late taxi in Lerici
July 2016**

What Not to Do in Rome (or Anywhere)

It was another stressful travel day. We lugged all of our suitcases down that small Lerici alleyway to the main square, where we waited for a taxi at the taxi stand. We waited and we waited. Finally one came, but it was too small for us, so the driver said that he had called a bigger one, and left.

We waited—and we waited. Once again, we found ourselves stressing out about trying to make a train on time. This was becoming an unhealthy habit—and we had only been in Italy for a week.

The taxi pulled up at 9:32 a.m. Our train was due to leave Spezia station at 10:06 a.m., which was 20 minutes away from Lerici. We arrived at the station at 10:00 a.m., and the five of us—like a frenetic traveling circus—scrambled to the platform by 10:05 a.m. We made it!

The train ended up being thirty minutes late.

This was just what we needed—more waiting with the kids, in the heat. Fun.

The train ride to Rome was painful in many ways. It was the five of us and one Italian woman, sitting in a compartment that had subpar air conditioning, for three hours. At last, we pulled into Roma Termini train station.

We managed to get the kids and luggage out to the front of the station and from there we planned to take a taxi to our apartment. Excitement was creeping in as we were close to our destination—until we saw that the line for taxis stretched around the corner and thought, "Oh please, not more waiting, with the kids, in the heat!"

Before we could get to the end of the line, we saw a very nice, rather large Italian man who was walking up and down the line asking people if they needed a ride. He said he was a taxi driver and had a van across the street. We looked at each other with doubting glances, but the thought of waiting in that heat with the kids moved us past our doubts.

Nine out of ten times, my wife and I would have ignored a random man like this in a country outside of the U.S.—especially being from New York. Yet in this instance, the morning travel had pushed our patience limits. He proceeded to lead us—not just across the street, but also around the corner.

Remember, there were five of us—and our luggage. We were already having second thoughts; they worsened when he pointed to his black van.

As we got in, I couldn't help but think, "What the hell are we doing?"

I could tell my wife was thinking the same thing. I started talking to him, asking him questions like, "Are you off-duty? What hours do you typically work? How far from Rome do you drive people?" I also looked around his car, searching for items like taxi driver identification—which I did eventually see. His name was Agostino and he ended up being a nice, funny man.

This photo shows the kids and me at the front door of our Rome apartment which was located in a very narrow alleyway that our taxi driver skillfully navigated.

We gave him the address to our apartment and he took us on a ride we'll never forget. We drove through the streets of Rome until we arrived at a very narrow alleyway, where he said, "Your apartment is down there."

I was thinking that he was going to let us out so we could walk, but he announced, "Hold on." For the next few minutes, he somehow weaved his van through the narrowest of Italian alleys and pulled up at the front door of our apartment. There was so little room that we could barely open the van doors.

Once again, against all odds, we had made it—this time to the Eternal City.

In Awe of the Colosseum

We quickly settled into our apartment which was right in the heart of Rome. Unfortunately, both the air conditioning and washing machine were not working, so that feeling of stickiness on our skin seemed likely to be with us for our entire stay in the city.

In keeping with the theme of our trip so far, we didn't rest at all. We freshened up, took a quick look at a map, and decided to take what would be another long walk to find il Coliseo, known in English as the Colosseum.

We took a wrong turn, which added 15 minutes to our already exhausting walk, but then we saw it. It was another one of those *"This is why we travel"* moments.

The kids were again in awe, just like when they saw

the Leaning Tower of Pisa. It seemed like every time exhaustion or frustration crept in during our trip, a sight like the Colosseum would overpower it.

We spent nearly an hour inside the Colosseum, staring in wonder at every aspect of this grand structure. Looking back, it was probably the best possible first location to visit in Rome, because it really represents the history of the city.

Our visit to the Colosseum on the evening we arrived in Rome.

We eventually walked back to our apartment, stopping at the market to pick up some food. At home, we cooked dinner with our fresh finds and passed out in the humidity.

It was another very long day—which I would soon realize was actually the norm for Italians.

Jubilee Year at the Vatican

The next day we had a tour of the Vatican booked. It was set to start early in the afternoon and last for about three hours.

The first mistake we made was deciding to walk to the Vatican—and make a stop at the Pantheon on the way. This was another beginner family traveling mistake: don't go on long walks in the heat before an extended tour.

By the time we made it to the Vatican, the kids were exhausted. Our tour guide, Mattea, was from the area and really did give us a wonderfully detailed tour. It was definitely too detailed for the kids, but we learned a lot about how the Vatican works.

What made this trip to the Vatican special was that it was during a Jubilee year. A Year of Jubilee, also called a Holy Year in the Roman Catholic Church, is a celebration that is observed on particular special occasions. Traditionally, it only occurs for one year in every 25.

However, it can also be celebrated when a special indulgence is granted to members of the faith by the Pope and confessors are given special faculties, including the lifting of censures. In this case, the Jubilee year was one such special event, enacted by Pope Francis in an effort to inspire Roman Catholics to be more merciful in their ways.

It was a unique gift to be able to visit the Vatican during this time. There is a "Holy Door" or 'Porta Sancta' in Saint Peter's Basilica at the Vatican which is only open during a Jubilee or Holy Year. On the first day of a holy year, the Pope strikes the brick wall with a silver hammer and opens the door to the people. Being able to walk through and touch the Holy Door was truly special.

Our son AJ with his favorite part of the Vatican City tour in the background, The Swiss Guard.

The highlight of the tour for the kids was learning about and seeing the changing of the Swiss Guard. My son still remembers more about the rules for becoming a Swiss Guard than anything else he learned on the entire 40-day trip.

One Too Many Trips

We finished up our time in Rome with a nice birthday dinner for my son, at an excellent restaurant that had gluten-free options for him. Be warned, eating out in Rome is very expensive, especially with a family of five.

The next morning we were packed and ready to head to Sorrento, the last stop before we would finally meet our family. Agostino, our mysterious cab driver, showed up on time, again navigating his way through the alleys to pull up right at our front door. He dropped us off at Roma Termini Station, where, for the first time on the trip, we were early for the train. We were finally getting the hang of this traveling thing.

Our venture would include a train ride from Rome to Naples, a cab ride to the ferry, a ferry to Sorrento, and lastly a cab ride to our apartment. Another travel mistake that hopefully you can learn from.

We got off the train in Naples, and there was a gentleman standing there with a taxi sign saying that he would drive us to our apartment in Sorrento for $100. Rather than taking his offer, we decided to stick with the original plan of taking the ferry since we had already booked it. Mistake.

We instead asked this man to take us to the ferry. He passed us off to one guy, who passed us off to another guy, who walked us through a pharmacy and out the back of the train station to his little Fiat. We started getting nervous again and had flashbacks to the taxi driver in Rome, but that had turned out ok.

Even though our experiences with unaccredited taxi and Uber drivers were relatively safe, take caution if you try to hire a driver who does not have proper affiliations, as while these may appear to save some time and money, they could put you in harm's way.

So in the midst of a busy road, with our driver, Gennaro, smoking in our faces, we crammed into his Fiat. (Just a side note here: it seemed that every man in Naples was named Gennaro, so I looked into this and found some interesting information on Wikipedia. Gennaro is the Italian form of the Roman cognomen *Ianuarius,* from "January" in Latin. The name of the month derives from the name of the Roman god Janus. Saint Gennaro, the patron saint of Naples, was a bishop who was beheaded during the persecutions of Emperor Diocletian in the fourth century.)

Gennaro drove us to the ferry while he spoke to us in a dialect from which I could barely pick up a few words.

He dropped us off in the middle of a busy road, and then, of course, wanted more money than we gave him; that part I understood.

We waited and boarded the boat for what was the choppiest ferry ride I've ever experienced. Our youngest daughter Penelope got sick and vomited all over the boat. Boy, do I wish we had paid that taxi driver $100 to take us right to our apartment.

Lesson learned. Take the most direct route to your destination—especially when traveling with kids—even if it costs more money.

Benvenuto a Sorrento (Welcome to Sorrento)

Sorrento is a beautiful city, or as they would say in Italian, "una bella città."

We walked around the city for a while and ended up finding a wonderful salumeria (deli), right near our apartment, where I had my first encounter with mozzarella di bufala. I was in love.

Mozzarella di bufala (buffalo mozzarella) is a mozzarella made from the milk of the domestic Italian water buffalo. It is traditionally produced in the Campania region of Italy, especially in the provinces of Caserta and Salerno.

I have been eating mozzarella for all of my life, and my wife is from Brooklyn (where they have some very good mozzarella)—but never had I tasted anything like this. For the next few days, we would regularly have a healthy supply of this indulgence in our apartment, along with some fresh tomatoes, green olives, and wine from the area around the local volcano Mount Vesuvius (Monte Vesuvio).

Sorrento is a beautiful coastal city with a really fun and lively downtown consisting of alleyways jammed with tourists and vendors. We settled in, but again, there was no rest for the weary as we would travel to Pompeii the next morning.

We were now only days away from meeting my relatives and I could barely contain my excitement. I honestly had no idea what to expect, which made for a very curious energy in the final days of this leg of the trip. No matter what sights we saw, the impending reunion was constantly on my mind.

Pompeii in the Rain

In keeping with our travel practice, we didn't sleep late our first day in Sorrento; we got up early and headed out to Pompeii for a guided tour that we had booked before leaving the U.S.

Pompeii is a large archaeological site, located in the southern Campania region. At one time it was a thriving Roman city, until in 79 A.D., when the village was buried in meters of ash and pumice after the catastrophic eruption of Mount Vesuvius. Today this well-preserved site, near the coast of the Bay of Naples, features excavated ruins that tourists can freely explore.

If you haven't been to Pompeii and plan to visit the Campania region of Italy, it's worth a stop—and I highly recommend a tour. There are so many facts and stories about this village that are best understood in the moment, explained by a guide. One of the most interesting features, as scary as it sounds, is seeing the remains of people who were buried in the ash during the eruption, as this coating preserved them from the heat and magma. These can be seen in a few different locations in Pompeii.

Again, the tour was probably information overload for the kids—but they at least had fun running around.

One of the biggest takeaways for me had nothing to do with Pompeii, but was from a conversation with our tour guide Paola about the mozzarella di bufala. She told me that the locals keep the cheese on their counter in a bag of salt water for up to 7 days and use it a little at a time. After seven days they refrigerate it. I know, typical Italian—I go to Pompeii and what I remember is the tour guide talking about mozzarella.

Towards the end of our Pompeii tour, it rained for the one and only time during our entire 40-day trip. The skies turned dark and gloomy over this ancient village and the rains came down. My son got scared and we all huddled beneath one of the ruins with Paola.

We finally decided to brave the downpour and take the train back to Sorrento. Though we did not climb to the top of the volcano Mount Vesuvius, if you are interested, it is an option that we heard great things about.

We would, however, climb a different volcano before the end of our trip.

Our family with one of the preserved victims of the Vesuvius Eruption.

The Secluded Cove Adventure

When you're in Italy, or anywhere for that matter, it's easy to travel to big cities and do all of the things tourists usually do. However, what I have found really makes a trip exciting is taking adventures to places that you would never normally visit.

We had now been in Italy for almost two weeks, with three young children, in very small apartments—we needed an adventure. While good Wi-Fi proved extremely hard to find in Italy, we were lucky that the Wi-Fi in our Sorrento apartment was reasonable, so my wife and I went online to find something creative and exciting we could do with the kids.

We read some great articles about a secluded cove which was about a 30-minute walk from downtown Sorrento. The cove was called the Bagni della Regina Giovanna (Queen Giovanna baths), and the articles online described it as a fun day trip destination.

The next morning, with a backpack full of food and snacks and a rough idea of where the cove was, the five of us set out.

First of all, we underestimated the difficulty of taking a 30-minute walk with three kids in the heat. What was worse, at some points in the walk, there was no sidewalk. Yes, it was scary and yes, it was yet another mistake, but we made it. The cove was really beautiful and not terribly crowded. The water was rough, but overall the experience was another confidence boost for us. To know that, even with three young kids, we could venture off and create our own memories was such a positive feeling.

We stayed for a while and ate our lunch, which consisted of peanut butter (burro di arachidi) and banana on rice cakes, and then headed home. On the way back, we decided to stop in town and book ourselves a day trip to Capri for the next day.

This would be the last stop before we drove to meet our family.

Our oldest daughter Brianna (with eyes closed) with the Bagni della Regina Giovanna cove behind her.

Capri—My Favorite Island Ever

It was another early morning in Sorrento, and another adventure—this time to the beautiful island of Capri.

As we rushed to get the kids ready to catch our bus for the ferry, we were now one day away from meeting the family. I had to remind myself stay focused on today though, and enjoy every moment we had in this beautiful country.

The ferry ride to Capri was, as you would imagine, absolutely breathtaking, with views of the mountainous cliffs and caverns tucked along the side of Capri. We stopped in both the white and green grottos (caves), but unfortunately couldn't visit the blue grotto because it was flooded with water due to the recent heavy thunderstorms. The boat also cruised under the tunnel of love (tunel di amore), a beautiful rock formation in the middle of the water.

When we got to Capri, we went straight to the beach—the Marina Grande. Not only was it beautiful, but also it was the clearest water I've ever swum in. I saw thousands of fish with my snorkel gear. It was one of those experiences where you really never want to come out of the water, and we never wanted to leave. I've been to a lot of beaches in a lot of places—but this was easily one of my absolute favorites.

Forty Days in Italy Con La Mia Famiglia

My kids and I before we go through the Tunel di Amore (just to the right of my son's visor).

We eventually took the elevated tram to the other side of the island where we walked through some of the very expensive shops. The shopping wasn't very interesting to us, but there was one vendor whom I remember vividly. He was a man in his fifties sitting in front of his small outdoor shop. He had a typical island look about him; he wore shorts, flip-flops, and no shirt.

He was sitting in front of an easel, painting a beautiful landscape. He was surrounded by his other paintings, all of which were for sale. I remember telling my wife, "This is what I want to do one day." I regret not purchasing one of his paintings, although maybe I was subconsciously giving myself a reason to return to Capri.

We headed back to the ferry for another beautiful (but more choppy) ride back to Sorrento. We grabbed a quick dinner, got the kids to bed, and packed up for the next leg of our trip. From this point on, we would be with family—in a way we've never been before.

Lessons Learned in Rome and Sorrento

Here are some lessons learned from the second leg of our trip in Rome and Sorrento, in the hopes our mistakes can save you some time and frustration.

Be wary of random people offering you a ride in their 'taxis.'

Even though it worked for us on this trip, don't just be quick to jump in anyone's car like we did. Try to verify that they are either a legitimate taxi or Uber driver.

Consider booking your tours in the U.S.

They can be extremely educational, so give yourself the time (and good Wi-Fi) to research the best ones. Otherwise, you might get duped into a bad deal on the streets. Also, if traveling with children, consider shorter tours more focused on big picture items instead of details.

Minimize the number of modes or legs of transportation during your trip.

I can't reinforce this point enough. It may be slightly more expensive to take a taxi as opposed to a bus and ferry or other combination, but the increased cost will be saved in frustration and exhaustion.

Talk to locals as much as possible about culture, food, traditions, etc.

This will make your experience so much richer and give you an unrehearsed and authentic perspective on such things.

Take non-touristy adventures every so often, like our walk to the secluded cove.

These will keep you energized and allow you to connect even more deeply with the culture and the local experience.

Do what's fun for you.

We could have spent a lot more time exploring the different parts of Capri, but we found an amazing beach and just felt like staying there. No regrets.

You can download a list of these lessons learned, and find other helpful resources, at FortyDaysInItaly.com.

Chapter 8

La Mia Famiglia

Just after getting to our apartment in Paestum, I find myself looking at a message on my phone from my cousin, Maria Rosa: "We'll pick you up at 8 p.m. for dinner."

Chills run through my body. Two years of research, travel planning, learning Italian—and now we are just hours away from the moment of truth.

What will they be like? What will their home be like? What will the food be like?

Will it be just like the stories you always hear of warm Italian families tucked away in these small villages in the mountains of Italy? Unlimited amount of local meals, wines, desserts—and most importantly, smiles and laughs. Will the stories be true?

We are about to find out.

**Standing in our apartment in Paestum, Italy,
hours from meeting my Italian relatives
July 2016**

The Drive and Detour to Family

We woke up early the last morning in Sorrento and packed up our luggage. Well, Jill did most of the packing, and I took a walk to pick up our first rental car of the trip.

The plan was to drive to our next stop, Paestum, where we would spend about five days. While there, we would visit our family who live on a farm in the hills of a small nearby village named Albanella. We kept the car until we left for Sicily from Napoli Airport six days later. So much would happen in those six days.

The drive to Paestum from Sorrento, if done straight through and with no traffic, is only about two hours. However, neither of those hypothetical scenarios held true for us. Not only did we hit a lot of traffic, but, also, I had the bright idea of stopping in Sarno, the birthplace of my great-grandparents (my mother's maternal grandparents). I wanted to try to obtain some records.

Jill kept asking me, "Did you call them? Are you sure the records office is open?" I tried looking on the website, but it was too difficult to understand, so I just brushed her comments off and said, "It will be open."

We finally arrived in the small village of Sarno, which lies at the foot of the Apennine Mountains. It was about 2 p.m., and the main street was entirely empty. Of course, my wife was staring at me, not saying, but I am sure thinking, "You didn't call, did you?" We found our way to the village hall, known in Italy as il Comune. Sure enough, they had closed for the day and told me to come back tomorrow.

This was another mistake that I take the blame for—but it was also our introduction to the Italian siesta. This a period of at least three hours during the afternoon where these villages completely shut down. I mean, the place was literally a ghost town.

Upon returning home to the U.S., I did some research on this and found a great article on *The Huffington Post* written by Marta Mondelli entitled, "Quality of Life: The Italian Siesta."

> *What do the Italians do when they close their stores? Many people think that they go home and take a nap, a siesta (Spanish word, by the way). This is one of the Italian myths we never cared to explain. If you are the owner of a store (granted you can resist the chains, the franchises, the malls, and the economic crisis), let's say you have a clothing store in the city center: you open the gate at around 9 a.m. till 12.30 p.m., then you go home, you cook, eat, rest a little (I doubt you'd nap: it depends on how close your apartment and your store are) and then you come back at about 3.30 and finally close for the day approximately at 7 p.m.*

That's quality of life: sacrificing the possibility of making some business for the tranquility of having a nice home-cooked meal. I know it's great to be able to buy what you need at any time and it's actually a real pain to realize it's Sunday and the only thing you can do is window shop. But, before moving to New York, that was my life: it's easy to adjust to these rhythms, especially if everybody around you comes back home and cooks and is not out there shopping or gulping a panino during lunch break.

This is my oldest daughter Brianna and me during siesta time in Sarno, motioning, "Where is everyone?"

When we first encountered this siesta period, which my wife and I referred to as a 'shutdown,' we were frustrated. By the time we left southern Italy, however, I wished we had the siesta back in the U.S.

Lesson learned. We eventually made it down to our hotel in Paestum, a nice, but not modern or touristy, part of Italy.

For the first time on our trip, I felt like we were in a location that could be truly referred to as "Southern Italy." The Southern Italy that I had heard so many of our guests on *The Italian American Podcast*, like Gay Talese, refer to. These villages weren't fancy, but they were home to our ancestors.

Of course, our apartment complex was also closed for siesta when we arrived, so we went to a local market until the caretaker came back at 4 p.m. We unpacked, and I texted back and forth with my cousin whom we had come to visit.

Maria Rosa Salese was about my age, and our great-grandfathers, Germano and Angelo, were brothers. They both came to the United States in the early 1900s. Germano, my great-grandfather (my father's maternal grandfather) liked it and stayed. Angelo didn't like it and so returned to the family farm in Albanella.

We were about to visit the family farm that I had heard so much about.

The Moment of Truth: La Mia Famiglia

Around 8 p.m., I get a text from Maria Rosa, saying "Siamo qui," which means, "We are here." A weird feeling came over me, specifically in my stomach. Happiness, nervousness, and what-the-heck-are-we-doing-here—all rolled into one.

I think we were all excited but had no idea what to expect, and it was late for the kids after a long day of travel. We walked downstairs, exited the apartment complex, and there they were.

Maria Rosa Salese is a pretty young woman who could have been in my place, and me in hers, if it had been my great-grandfather that didn't like America. Next to her was her father Aldisio, a short but stocky man. When you looked at him, the words 'strong' and 'farmer' came to mind; we would later confirm that he was both.

The whole exchange was pleasant, and then we saw their car—a small Fiat. Jill and I were both thinking the same thing: "How are seven of us fitting in that little car?"

After some maneuvering and conversing, using my average Italian (which would improve dramatically over the next few weeks), we all ended up in that little car. I sat in the front with Aldisio, while Jill and kids sat in the back with Maria Rosa.

La Mia Famiglia

Myself and our kids with Maria Rosa and Aldisio, at the farm on the drive up to their house for dinner the first evening.

I continued to hold my own with my Italian during the 15-minute ride through the hills up to their farm. As we got close, we made a few stops and they showed us the property—including a religious shrine they had built and a series of wind turbines that the city had installed. Their property sat at the top of a mountain.

They referred to the wind turbines as turbini (tur-be-nee) in Italian. The nice thing about the turbines was that, for the rest of the trip, we could see them from our hotel, so the kids always knew where the family was. They also helped us to find the place again on our own.

I couldn't believe it, but we had made it to one of the places where it all started.

The Dinner I Will Never Forget

It was late, and I knew this visit with the family would challenge the kids.

Luckily, there was a couch next to the dining area, on which the kids would crash soon after we got there. The house was pretty much what I expected—a modest home on a farm. Not too big, but big enough to house them and allow them to successfully run the farm, which was their source of sustenance.

Dinner with the Salese family in the hills of Albanella on the first night we arrived.

We were in the dining room—a long room with an equally long table where we all sat. The evening, while a bit awkward at times (maybe because of the language barrier and the difference in cultures), was nonetheless everything you would imagine it to be.

I had heard stories of Italian Americans finding and visiting their Italian relatives, and they all seemed to suggest that the Italians were very warm and hospitable. They would feed their guests feasts consisting of large homemade meals (including wine) and welcome them in with open arms. Well, I can honestly say this evening, and our entire stay with the Salese family, followed everything that I had heard.

After some small talk, they started bringing out the food, course by course. This is what I wrote in my diary:

1st course: prosciutto, capicola, mozzarella di bufala, cantaloupe, and bread.

2nd course: rice, corn, peppers, peas and tuna with a tomato carved into a decorative flower garnish. Served with water and homemade wine.

3rd course: watermelon.

4th course: ice cream, cookies, and espresso. The kids woke up for this course.

5th course: a digestif.

Practically everything that we ate was made from the food grown at their farm, with the exception of the mozzarella (which was delivered), the wine (which Aldisio's brother had made), and a few other items.

We went back and forth conversing, mostly about our family history, and they even showed me some photos of my great-grandfather's brother Angelo.

Eventually, we carried the kids to the Fiat, and Aldisio drove us back to our apartment. We arrived at midnight, and as tired as I was, it was difficult sleeping that night. I knew this was a once-in-a-lifetime experience.

Going Back to Sarno: il Comune

In keeping with the theme of our trip, we woke up early the next morning and were on the road again. This time, we had planned to take a day trip back to Sarno, the village of my maternal grandmother's parents, Giuseppe Baselice and Mary Paciullo.

Even though my grandmother did have pretty good information about her parents, there were some questions that I was hoping to answer. I also really wanted to visit their village and learn as much as I could about it.

After all, when someone asks, "Where are you from," Sarno would be one of my answers. I felt a duty to my great-grandparents to be able to answer that question with much more detail than just "Italy." Especially when the question was posed by my own children—and eventually, if I am lucky enough, grandchildren.

The one positive about visiting Sarno during the siesta the day before, even though the Comune was closed, was that we were now familiar with the layout of the town. We parked and walked back to the Comune, bringing all of the records that I had brought from my grandmother. I went up to the records window and explained, in Italian, what I was looking for.

The man looked at my documents, put them down on the desk, and asked me to come back in 30 minutes. Okay, that felt like progress.

During that half hour, we walked through the village of Sarno. Walking through a small village where your great-grandparents grew up over one hundred years ago is something not everyone has the chance to do.

We went into some small markets and simply observed the locals in their daily activities of shopping and conversing with one and another. Most who were working in the stores stared at us, like we were strangers, until I explained why we were there. Then they became super friendly and asked me about my great-grandparents, their names, etc.

I found this to be the case in all of these origin villages; they appreciated that we were coming back to learn about our roots. Then, something interesting happened.

First, you should know that my grandmother (now 90 years old), still hosts our entire family every year on

Easter Saturday, as she has done for years. One of my favorite dishes that she makes is a pasta pie. It is made of pasta, egg, and pieces of ham. Delicious. It was a specialty of her mother, Maria Paciullo. It became an Easter staple in our family, and we only have it a few times a year—which is part of what makes it so special.

While we were walking through Sarno, we walked into a small salumeria (deli). I looked through the different foods behind the glass at the counter, and I saw it: my great-grandmother Mary's pasta pie. I got goosebumps. Who would imagine finding the pie you grew up with in the small village in Italy where your great-grandma was from?

It looked exactly the same as the one my grandmother had been making for years. Of course, I asked for a piece, and we walked to the park, where I took a bite. It was our pie. It tasted exactly the same as if my grandmother had made it. Unbelievable. As much as I was still hoping to find paper records of my ancestors in the Comune, to me, this was the ultimate confirmation that I had found my Italian roots. If you do visit your ancestral village in Italy, look for the foods that you grew up with.

We headed back to the Comune. The gentleman, who had taken my papers, now led me to another room where a man and woman were sitting. He handed the

La Mia Famiglia

man my papers, basically as if he had done nothing the entire time I was gone.

It seemed like it was going to be a lengthy process, so Jill took the younger kids out to the street to play and my oldest daughter, Brianna, stayed with me. The man looked at my records and, based on the last name and birth or death year (if they died in Italy), he pulled out these big books to look for their birth and death certificates.

We did very well in that room.

My oldest daughter Brianna with the record keeper in the Sarno Comune.

He found the birth certificates of both sets of my great-grandparents—but then we took it one step further. My grandma had always told me that her grandparents (her father's parents) had been killed during the battle of Salerno in 1943. So I tried it. I gave the man her grandparent's names and the death year of 1943, and he found the death certificate of her grandfather Aniello Baselice. Unbelievable. It had so much information on it.

After we left the Comune, we went to a coffee shop where we spoke to the owner for an hour; it turned out that he knew more of my relatives. In fact, one of them stopped by the coffee shop—a female cousin of mine who was a lawyer in town.

If you go to your ancestral villages in Italy, be sure that in addition to visiting the Comune, you go to a local coffee shop, explain why you are there, and give your relative's name. Most likely, someone will have some information for you.

It was another long and hot day, but again I felt like I was making so much progress. As I collected more pieces of the puzzle that is my history, the answer to the question, 'Where did I come from?' was getting clearer.

> *I have to mention one sad note here. It was on this day that I also found out that my grandfather Serafino (Sal) Piraneo passed away in the U.S., at age 90. He had been sick with liver cancer for six months or so by this time, but this was the first grandparent I had lost. Honestly, I couldn't really process the news because of everything else going on with the trip,*

including taking care of the kids. All I could do was tell myself that he had lived a good, long life, and that he would be proud that in a few weeks I would be visiting the town of Sortino where his parents grew up—yet which he had never had the chance to visit.

The Moment All Italian Americans Live For

The next day I woke early, left Jill and the kids at the apartment, and drove to the family's farm. Aldisio had agreed to drive with me to Controne, a small village 20 minutes away, where my great-grandfather Antonio Fasano was born. As his namesake, I felt an obligation to learn about this man.

I sat in the small Fiat, next to Aldisio, and there were about 10 different feelings running through me—among them excitement, nervousness, anxiety, and disbelief. This day would prove to be one that stood out from many of the other days on this trip.

The car ride consisted of some small talk in my conversational-at-best Italian with my cousin, whom I had only met earlier that week. Even though our communication wasn't perfect, we both knew the importance of this trip, and Aldisio seemed to be as determined as me to find out about this figure who meant so much—Antonio Fasano.

Controne is a small village in the province of Salerno, in the region of South-Western Italy. In 2010, its population was 873. It was a half-hour ride through the rolling hills of Salerno. Up and down, orchard after orchard, and then finally we arrived…

Aldisio pulled into the driveway of the first house we saw, which sat next to a small yellow church. He left the car, went up to the door, and knocked.

A woman came out, and they engaged in a short conversation, during which he pointed at me several times. The woman went back inside to get her car keys and we followed her to a house about two minutes down the street.

As we pulled up to the house, I saw the name FASANO on the driveway sign post. Immediately, I got goosebumps again. We got out of our cars, and the woman called up to a balcony, explaining to the woman upstairs who we were. Without hesitation, the woman, named Lelianna, invited us into her house.

It was only she and an older woman there at the time, but she invited us to sit down in her kitchen and immediately offered us food and drink. I didn't think about it at the time, but the trust these people had, to let two men whom they never met before into their house, was wonderful.

Her husband, Antonio Fasano, showed up a few minutes later. I am still not sure how he knew we were there, as she didn't make a phone call, but apparently news in small villages in southern Italy travels quickly.

This man, who was a very welcoming and kind man, came up to me, put out his hand, and said, "Sono Antonio Fasano," which meant, I am Anthony Fasano. I shook his hand, and repeated, "Sono Antonio Fasano." We both smiled and laughed.

He went into the formal dining room and took a letter off the table and held it up as if to say, "I knew you were coming." It was a letter I had written him about six months earlier, explaining who I was and that I was coming to find out about my great-grandfather who shared my name.

Until he showed me the letter, I had no idea that I had sent it to him specifically. I just sent it to anyone with the name Fasano in the area, as I mentioned in Chapter 2. We talked for a short time, with the help of Aldisio, and found out that we are distant cousins. This is when it got interesting.

Aldisio, Antonio, and I got into the Fiat. I had no idea where we were going, but we ended up in the Comune, or Village Hall. We went to the records department, and Antonio told me to give them the information about my great-grandfather. I had a birth date for him of 1892. I also had information that he arrived in the United States in 1912, at the age of 23.

After looking through a few different books based on his birth year of 1892, they found nothing, and my excitement started to turn to fear. Did I come all this way for nothing? Would I not be able to confirm my name came from this small village in the mountains?

Then, all of a sudden, Aldisio and Antonio started pointing to my notes and saying to the man behind the counter "mille-ottocento-ottanta-nove" (1889). They said it repeatedly and with excitement. They had realized that if my great-grandfather was 23 in 1912, he would have been born in 1889, not 1892.

They opened the book and flipped through the pages slowly, with all of us anxiously waiting. Antonio soon began pointing and said, "Ecco qua." I knew enough Italian to realize this was it. They had found it: Antonio Giorgio Fasano, born on November 12, 1889, in Controne, Italy.

I would later realize that not only was it rare for Italians to have middle names but that no one in my family knew he had a middle name—which is probably why there are no Giorgios in my family. (Yet.) They wouldn't give me a copy of the birth certificate, but they did allow me to take a photo. The three of us went to the bar next door for a celebratory drink.

Then I really hit the jackpot.

We got back in the car, and the two men were so excited at this point that their already heavy dialects became even more difficult to understand. I assumed we were going to take Antonio home, but then we made a turn up a mountainous road. After about two minutes, the car stopped, and they both got out.

They looked at me, and it took a few minutes for me to figure out what they were saying. "This is the street where your great-grandfather was born," they told me.

Here I am on the street where Antonio Fasano was born in 1889.

We walked up and down the street and, although the specific house number indicated on the birth certificate no longer seemed to be there, it was still special.

I found what I believe every Italian American dreams of—the exact location where their name comes from.

We dropped Antonio off at his home, where he said to me repeatedly, "Cena Venerdi. Cena Venerdi," inviting my family and me to dinner at his home on Friday. I can honestly say that if I had traveled all the way to Italy from New Jersey, and all I had got to experience was this one trip to Controne, it would have been worth it.

This Family Doesn't Need Fancy

The next few days with family in Albanella were wonderful. The kids really enjoyed spending time on the farm with the animals, and it was amazing to me how the family of four, plus Aldisio's mother, operated the vast farmland.

The only product that they sell from their farm produce is olive oil; however, they grow and produce many other items, including fruits (like figs, cantaloupe, and watermelon), meats (like chicken and prosciutto), cheeses (including goat cheese), and so much more. They had about 40 cows, 20 goats, and more chickens than I could count. It seemed to be so much work for them, day and night—but it also seemed normal for them.

It seemed to me that the community works to support each other. They produce way too much food for themselves, but from our conversations, I gathered that they share it with other family members in town and get other items in return—like the wine and mozzarella. This is how the Italian immigrant neighborhoods worked when my great-grandparents moved here, but not anymore.

The next night, we went for dinner at Aldisio's sister's home. It was an interesting house that contained a cigarette store which his sister Alida ran. She lived in the house with her daughter, son-in-law, and grandchild. Of course, her other son, sister-in-law, and two grandchildren lived upstairs in another apartment; typical Italian setup.

Dinner outdoors with the Salese family at Aldisio's sister's house.

This gathering to me really stressed the simplicity of their lives as compared to ours. It was held on a nothing-fancy, concrete patio, that was covered in a turf grass carpet, behind the house. A basic open brick fireplace was used for cooking. Simple, delicious foods were consumed; not necessarily simple to prepare, but things like peppers and other fresh vegetable salads. Sausages were cooked over the fire and a stack of pizzas were delivered.

It was an enjoyable and light atmosphere, and our kids had so much fun with their newfound young cousins. None of them had a worry in the world. This is how life should always be.

Everyone was so sincere and I felt like I had known them all for a long time. Once again, I felt like I was home.

Two Families Coming Together in the Mountains

It was now our last day before we were due to head to Sicily to meet the other side of our family. Our only plans for this day were to head over to the farm around 6 p.m., at which time Aldiso would drive us over to the Fasano's in Controne for dinner as we promised. Cena, Venerdi.

After a day at the beach, we packed our luggage, since we had an early flight the next morning, and headed back to the farm. Once there, we piled into the good old Fiat—but this time I got to experience that rolling ride to Controne with Jill and the kids.

The Fasanos were ready for us this time. Antonio warmly greeted us at the door, and he immediately took to the kids. He spoke such a slurred dialect, yet it seemed that we all knew exactly what he was saying—even my four-year-old, Penelope. I guess some people just have the ability, between their actions and personality, to communicate with anyone.

Along with his wife, he gave us a tour of their house. Then he showed us his garden and animals outside, helped the kids pick strawberries, and let them wash them with the hose and eat them.

My son and me with Antonio Fasano in front of his house.

He offered to drive us around the village for a tour—only he wasn't driving. Yes, you guessed it. Once again, we all piled into the now famous Fiat. This time our family of five shared the back seat. He gave us the tour, and pointed out great-grandpa Antonio's birthplace, where he'd taken me two days earlier.

As I sat there in the back seat of that Fiat, something struck me. Here I was, in the mountains of Southern Italy. Earlier that week, I had met my grandmother's family for the first time, and two days ago, I had found my grandfather's father's birthplace.

Now I had brought these two families together. Are you kidding me? If you would have told me 18 months ago that I was going to find living relatives in Italy, learn Italian, visit them, and have dinner with both Fasanos and Saleses in their villages, I would have laughed at you so hard that I would have injured myself.

We returned to Antonio's home, had a wonderful dinner, and then stopped back at the farm for one last late-night goodbye. What a week. What a trip so far.

Sicily, here we come.

Lessons Learned in Southern Italy

In keeping with my goal of this book to help you to create an experience like we had, here are some lessons learned from our time in southern Italy. Hopefully, they'll make your planning easier and your experience just as rich as ours:

When visiting Italian villages with an intent to visit the Comune and search for records, be sure to call ahead or visit the Comune website to make sure the records department will be open when you are there.

Also, keep in mind the Italian siesta—which usually happens between 12:30 pm and 4:00 pm.

If you are visiting Italian relatives, plan for very late dinners that start at 8 or even 9 p.m.

Also consider sleeping in or taking an afternoon nap so you can fully enjoy the dinner experience.

In small Italian villages, you can often ask questions of random people about your family or your family name and they will give you information.

Remember, in Controne, Aldisio knocked on the door of the first house we came to and the woman drove us to the Fasanos.

When in a Comune records department, furnish them with all of the information you have, even if it doesn't make sense to you.

Remember how I had my great-grandfather's birth date wrong? Aldisio and Antonio reviewed my notes and noticed my math error, meaning we were able to locate the birth certificate.

Don't necessarily expect fancy in southern Italy, but do expect authenticity.

I mean in regards to everything from the hotels and apartments to the homes and so on. After our experience, I wouldn't have it any other way.

Learning Italian will definitely enrich your experience in Italy, but even if you don't, you should still do everything you want to do.

People will find ways to communicate with you, just like Antonio did with us.

You can download a list of these lessons learned, and find other helpful resources, at FortyDaysInItaly.com.

Chapter 9

Sicilia Here We Come

It is only midday but it feels like midnight. It takes a lot of energy to get the kids to the airport on time, and then we have to deal with long lines and broken baggage carousels. We just barely make our flight.

The flight is relaxing, but short, and soon we land in Catania airport in Sicily. My mother's family, whom I had connected with about a year ago online, is driving an hour north to meet us for lunch. I have no idea what to expect.

In keeping with our travel troubles on the trip, our stroller is not on the baggage claim in Catania, but after an extra 10 to 15 minutes we find it.

As soon as we step into the airport, we see them. The family. All of them. They're there with a big welcome sign. All of the struggles from this morning vanish in one swift motion.

Once again, we feel like we are home.

Catania Airport
July 2016

A Warm Welcome to Sicily

Getting the kids up early (again) and traveling from Naples to Sicily was difficult. Packing and moving from one place to the next with three children really was the hardest part of the trip.

Napoli airport was extremely crowded; there were also mechanical problems with the belts that took the luggage from the check-in desk to the plane, which caused massive delays.

While both my father's and mother's families were from the Napoli region, my mom's father (Sal Piraneo, who had passed away just a few weeks earlier) was Sicilian. His mother and father came from a small village called Sortino, in the Siracusa region of south-western Sicily.

Francy Pagliaro, who was just a few years older than me, had connected with me on Facebook about a year ago after I sent handwritten letters to her mother, Nunzia. Francy's great-grandmother Alfia was the sister of my great-grandmother Rosina, who we referred to as Rose.

The entire family from Sortino was there, waiting for us, with a big welcome sign. It was exactly what we all needed after that morning. Again, it was that ability of Italian family to make you feel at home—and we needed it after our difficult travels.

Sicilia Here We Come

They took us to a wonderful restaurant in Catania where we had our first encounter with the Sicilian dish pasta alla norma (pasta with eggplant). They also gave us a walking tour of Catania and took the kids for gelato.

Nothing seemed to matter more to them then us whenever we were with them. In a world of a million distractions, that felt good. We bid them farewell, as we were off to Agrigento for a week, but we would reunite with them in one week's time.

*The family greeting us at the Catania Airport.
I am in the middle, with the hat, and Francy is to the right of me.*

By the Beach in Agrigento

We left Catania and drove three hours to Agrigento in south-eastern Sicily. We booked an apartment near the beach in San Leone, figuring this would be a part of the trip where we could relax for a few days with the kids and recharge.

Again, this was not an easy task with three excited children. "Relax" and "recharge" are words that are not in the vocabulary of young kids, especially my son, who we would find out (six months after we got back to the U.S.) has Attention Deficit Hyperactivity Disorder (ADHD).

It was a nice week in Agrigento; the beaches there are absolutely beautiful. My son and I went to the supermarket early each morning and got some mozzarella di bufala to make sandwiches for the beach.

While we were in the region, we visited a really beautiful spot called La Scala dei Turchi, which literally translates to Stairs (or Ladder) of the Turks. It is a rocky cliff on the coast near Porto Empedocle. It has become a tourist attraction due to the unusual white color of the stone, which is formed by marl (a sedimentary rock). The kids had a blast covering their body with this clay substance from the stone, which many people believe helps rejuvenate the skin.

In fact, the kids loved it so much that we went back for a second day. I noticed that most of the Italians who visited there hung out on the rocks for hours, just relaxing and taking in the sun. Tourists just came, climbed the rocks, and went home. I see this as a good analogy for the differences between Europeans and Americans; in my opinion, Europeans are much more relaxed.

My youngest child Penelope and me at La Scala dei Turchi on the white rocks.

Enna and the Temple

I can't say enough about taking day trips to small villages when you travel, whether it is in Italy or elsewhere.

I had heard a lot about the Sicilian village of Enna and so we decided to explore it one day. Enna is located in the center of Sicily; it offers stunning views, as it has one of the highest elevations in the area. Enna is also well-known for hosting the most elaborate holy week celebration in the world, which is comprised of several processions, over the course of the week, where citizens dress up and re-enact the past.

We saw some really beautiful churches and awe-inspiring views of Sicily, both in Enna and on the ride. On the ride back, we stopped at the Villa Romana del Casale, an estate near Armenia that contains the richest, largest, and most complex collection of Roman mosaics in the world. I highly recommend a visit there, if you make it to Sicily.

*My kids and me at the Valley dei Tempi.
You can see how hot they were here.*

The other attraction that we visited while in Agrigento was the Valle dei Tempi (which translates as the Valley of the Temples)—an archaeological site consisting of beautiful Greek ruins. It is one of the most outstanding examples of Greek art and architecture; it is also one of the main attractions of Sicily, as well as a national monument of Italy. I must warn you that it requires a decent amount of walking and is brutally hot on a sunny day.

Towards the end of our week in Agrigento, our family from the U.S. arrived and we were reunited with them. We would all spend the next week together in a villa in Trecastagni, Sicily for my uncle's birthday. After a wonderful week in Agrigento, we once again packed up and hit the road.

A Celebration of La Famiglia

Once again we drove across Sicily, this time to a villa in Trecastagni, which is in the north-east portion of the island.

We spent a week at this villa with relatives from the U.S.—including my parents, my brothers and their families, my Aunt Marie and Uncle Carl, and my Aunt Marie's family. The initial reason we had planned to be in Italy this summer was because Aunt Marie and Uncle Carl had invited us to this weeklong celebration.

The day we arrived was my Uncle Carl's actual birthday; there was a big party planned and we invited our Sicilian relatives from Sortino to join us. They had greeted us at the airport, the rest of my family would now get to meet them, and we would be able to start to build that familial connection.

The villa staff did a wonderful job of setting up a long table with beautiful Sicilian plates and glasses out in the yard. They also brought in a local chef—the food was amazing.

Our Sicilian family showed up and then the party really began (if you're judging by the volume of the conversations). When they met my family from the U.S. for the first time, it felt special to me, knowing that I had found them and facilitated this connection.

While I had already started to build the connection with my Sicilian cousin Francy online over the past year, and I had spent the day with her and the family in Catania a week ago, this night would be full of more hugging, talking in Italian, which greatly deepened the connection.

I started to realize that my cousin Francy Pagliaro and I seemed to have that kind of connection where you feel like you have known someone for years. We've referred to this on The Italian-American Podcast as 'blood memory.'

We had a wonderful night with everyone; I spent a lot of time talking with Francy and learning more about the differences between life in Italy and life in the U.S. I couldn't wait to spend more time with her during the next leg of our trip.

Francy and I on the porch of her summer home in front of a walnut (noci) tree.

A Visit to the Top of the Volcano

The week in the villa was even more of a low-key, "relax and recharge" week for us than Agrigento had been—and it was desperately needed. We spent most days by the pool and had some great family dinners cooked by the same local chef (including a pizza night where the kids made pizza with the chef).

Being the "on the move" type of people we are, we couldn't stay put all week. One day, Jill and I took our two older children to climb to the top of Mount Etna.

Mount Etna is an active volcano located between the cities of Messina and Catania, only a 30-minute ride from the villa. Etna is the tallest active volcano in Europe and is the highest peak in Italy south of the Alps.

Jill was still upset we hadn't climbed Mount Vesuvius near Pompeii weeks earlier, so we weren't going to miss out on this one.

To climb Mount Etna, you take a chairlift to a point about midway up the volcano, then a bus takes you closer to the top, and from there a tour guide walks with you the rest of the way. It is extremely windy and pretty cold at the top, even in the sweltering heat of summer. So if you go, be prepared.

The soaring views really take your breath away. My daughter's hat actually blew off the side of the mountain—but our tour guide climbed over and retrieved it, believe it or not. It was nice to get out, just the four of us, while our little one stayed at the villa with family.

Me and the kids at the top of Mount Etna. Bella vista!

Families Come Together for Pizza

During my Uncle's 60th birthday party, our relatives from Sortino invited us to drive down one night for pizza with all our family from the villa. It was about an hour away, and we all decided that it would be good to visit the town where Grandma Rose was born. Jill and I and the kids would be going for three days the following week, but this evening trip would give the rest of our family the opportunity to see one of our places of origin.

So we piled into two cars and headed to Sortino. We knew it was a small village when they told us to meet them at the "gate to the village" by the statue of la Madonna. We all joked about how we would never be able to say to them, "Just meet us at the main gate of New York City."

When we arrived, Nunzia and Auerilio, Francy's parents, were waiting for us. It was a beautiful statue, and Nunzia was suddenly really excited and speaking loudly in her Sicilian dialect. Both my Uncle and I were pretty good in Italian by this point, so we were able to understand what she was saying. She was telling us that the statue was built by the brother of my Grandpa Sal's grandfather; in other words, my maternal grandfather's grandfather's brother.

It took her a few times of saying, "il fratello di il nonno di tuo nonno," for me to put it together, but once I did, it was an amazing feeling. As I explained to you earlier, at home in New Jersey, I had done tons of family research. I had found all kinds of documentation, including birth certificates and draft cards—but never could I have found out something like this. Something so real and physical, something I wouldn't have been able to touch had I not travelled to Italy.

I stood there for a few minutes and took it all in. Then I hugged Nunzia.

My mother Rita, Nunzia, my Uncle Carl, and me in front of the statue of la Madonna—built by my great-great-grandfather's brother. Nunzia, my mom, and uncle share the same great-grandmother, Margherita Bucello.

Our next stop was Francy's summer house. It seems that many Italians have "summer homes" that are minutes away from their primary home. I must say, Francy's summer home may have been simple, but it was beautiful. The yard was loaded with olive trees, as well as a few fig trees with the freshest of figs—which I became addicted to.

This was a special gathering—one of those, stop, breathe, and take-it-all-in moments. We were all mingling and talking on this outdoor patio. You could hear family stories being shared in English, Sicilian, and Italian. This is why I came to Italy. Not for the fancy restaurants or the statues and monuments; it was for these simple moments of connection.

Eventually, they took us out for the best pizza we'd ever had. The pizzas included zucca (squash), salsiccia (sausage), pistachio, and ricotta cheese—and, of course, Nutella.

Another special night I will never forget.

Great Grandma Rosina's Home of Sortino

My grandfather Sal passed away only a few weeks ago. I remember his mother Rose only vaguely from when I was a very young child.

I remember she had a walker and spoke a language that was very difficult to understand—at the time I didn't know that it was a Sicilian dialect from her hometown of Sortino.

It is still hard to believe that we have found great-grandma Rose's sister's family in Sortino. It is even harder to believe I have been able to communicate with them for the last year, and that now we are going to spend three days in the village with them.

Is this all a dream? Is Grandpa watching? What will it be like?

Sortino… here we come.

My thoughts while driving to Sortino, Sicily, with my family
August 2016

Right to the River (il Fiume)

We enjoyed the rest of our time in the villa with our Italian American family members, but on Saturday morning we bid farewell and headed south to Sortino.

We would spend three days in Sortino, and most of that time would be spent with Francy, her husband Gianluca, and her children Mateo and Laura. We would also spend time with her brother Luigi, his girlfriend Rosanna, and new aunt and uncle, Nunzia and Aurelio.

We arrived in our rental car at the small village, where finding our apartment was a challenge. Sortino is a mountainous village consisting of very small (and, in some cases, one-way) alleys. We eventually found our apartment which, while inexpensive, was newly renovated and offered a beautiful balcony view of the mountains.

I took a walk outside and started to talk to several old Sicilian women who were sweeping their porches and driveways. I explained to them my family was from Sortino. They all asked for the family name, and when I told them Blancato and Pagliaro, they immediately knew who I was referring to. I can't help saying this once more—I felt like I had come home. Maybe it was that blood memory again.

We stayed in our apartment just long enough to put a few things away and then we were off to Francy's summer home. We started to feel an urgency about

Great Grandma Rosina's Home of Sortino

our time in Italy because we knew it was coming to an end. We wanted to spend as much time with la famiglia as possible. Monuments, churches, and other tourist attractions became secondary to conversations with my relatives.

These continued over a delicious lunch, prepared by Francy and Nunzia, on the porch of Francy's summer home. This would be a place of great conversations and connection over the next three days.

Newfound cousins connected by much more than just holding hands. This is one of my favorite pictures of the trip. My children are the three shortest.

Then they took us to a nearby river (il fiume). We had no idea what we were getting ourselves into, but it ended up being a 45-minute hike (in flip-flops) to a beautiful part of the river where our two families enjoyed swimming and laughing. Francy's son Mateo kept saying, "due minuti," indicating that we would be there in two minutes. He said that for half an hour, and it became a running joke during the rest of our time in Sortino.

This was a special excursion where our two families really bonded—especially the kids. The photo of our kids and Francy's children says it all: cugini (cousins). Age didn't matter; we were all family.

If you end up finding and visiting your family in Italy, arrange for experiences like this one where you just get away with your relatives, connect, and bond. What an afternoon.

Of course, we ended up back on Francy's porch that evening, cooking with the family. It was more than just a family-cooking gathering, as we learned about and cooked a pastry-like roll that contained a particular herb called Nepetella that only grows in Sortino. The roll is similar to a calzone but with much more flavor. When Gianluca's mother, who was Calabrese, took a bite out of the raw sausage, my 10-year old daughter looked at me, terrified.

I had to pinch myself again. I was with my family, on my relatives' outdoor porch in Sicily, cooking calzones. How did this happen?

Four Italian women and me making calzones; can you tell by my smile that I am in heaven? From left to right: Nunzia, Gianluca's sister, Francy, me, and Gianluca's mother.

A Tour to Remember Family (My Great-Great-Grandparents' Graves)

The next two days in Sortino, the family couldn't have been any more warm and welcoming.

The second day, they took us sightseeing to the beautiful town of Noto, and then to a nice beach nearby. On the beach, we enjoyed Arancini—a classic Sicilian food: stuffed rice balls which are coated with breadcrumbs and then deep-fried. They are usually filled with tomato sauce, mozzarella, and peas.

It was the third day in Sortino that hit home for me. Nunzia and Aurelio took us to the cemetery where my great-great-grandparents were buried. I simply can't describe the feeling and emotions going through me during this visit.

The cemetery was vast. In Sicily, the coffins are put into above-ground stone structures due to the water elevation. We walked through this cemetery in the heat and saw the family's names, Blancato and Pagliaro, on many stones; however, we eventually made it to the ones I was most eager to see.

From what I have heard, my great-great-grandmother Margherita Bucello was a strong woman. She used to sell fruit on the streets of Sicily and hide the money in a slot in a small wooden table. I don't know much about my great-great grandfather Serafino Blancato (who my grandfather was named after), but all indications were that he was a small yet strong person as well.

I climbed the portable steps with my son AJ and looked at the photo of Margherita and Serafino that was pinned onto the grave and touched it. It was amazing. Generations connected, at last.

Great Grandma Rosina's Home of Sortino

My son AJ and me at the grave of my great-great grandparents, Margherita Bucello and Serafino Blancato.

Nunzia then took us all over Sortino to meet other family members while also visiting some very important locations. We visited the location of the house where my great-grandfather Carlo Piraneo grew up, which was now a parking lot. We also visited the location of the house where my great-grandma Rose grew up, which is now a small eatery. Nunzia walked us through the eatery as she explained to us where the bathroom was, where they ate dinner, and where my grandma Rose slept. I felt once again like I had traveled back in time. Some sadness had crept in during this tour, as I couldn't help but think about how my grandpa Sal passed away just two weeks prior; I would never be able to tell him about this experience or show him the photos.

I didn't have to bother going to the Comune in Sortino to find family records, as Nunzia had already done that for me and handed me all of the papers during my visit. Her dedication was hard to believe and very touching.

There was no doubt that I had a special connection to this village and to Nunzia. Throughout our stay, she treated me as if she were a mother reunited with her long-lost son. There were so many times during these three days that, because of the language barrier, I shouldn't have been able to understand what she was saying to me—but our connection meant everything was crystal clear.

Lunch at Nunzia's house would follow, where Francy, Luigi, and their families joined us. Nunzia made the best eggplant parmigiana I ever had (but don't tell my grandma that).

Later that night, where do you think we ended up? Francy's porch for our last supper in Sortino, with just Francy's family and us—talking, reflecting, and connecting. I miss Francy and Nunzia a lot.

Great Grandma Rosina's Home of Sortino

The last supper in Sortino with Francy and her family, once again on the outdoor porch. Can it get more simple than this?

Goodbye to Sicily

Sadly, our time in Sicily had to come to an end. We woke early and loaded up the car, and I wasn't surprised to find out that Francy and her family were coming to the airport to see us off. They were there for us, from the second we landed until the second we departed. Famiglia.

We drove by the statue of La Madonna, built by my great-great-grandfather's brother, and I had to stop and get out and take a few last photos. I had come to learn the importance of this statue to the village over the last few days, and it now meant a lot to me too. People would gather by the statue at night and just relax together in its beauty. Also, every couple that was married in Sortino would visit the statue after the wedding for photos.

We left Sicily on my daughter Brianna's birthday. What a gift for her, being able to see her Sicilian relatives on that day. Francy, Gianluca, Mateo, and Laura gave us a very warm send-off.

We had one last stop on our trip. We would head back to Napoli for a few days to stay with my sister-in-law's family and take one last trip to the Salese farm to bid them farewell.

There is no doubt in my mind that I will reunite with Nunzia and Francy soon.

Time to Say Goodbye to Napoli

My brother Christopher's wife's parents come from an area close to Naples. He and his wife, Antonella, had headed back there to visit after leaving our villa in Trecastagni, and now we would spend a few days with them at the end of our trip.

It was another chance to experience how Italian families live so closely together. Antonella's family lived on various floors of one large apartment building.

The day we arrived was both my daughter Brianna's birthday and Chris and Antonella's anniversary, so the family planned a big party at a restaurant with a lot of people. It was nice, but, of course, our kids didn't make it to the end—which was after midnight.

The next day, we took a ride back to the Salese farm in Albanella; we had promised them that we would come and say goodbye. Of course, they had prepared a huge and delicious lunch for us to enjoy. After lunch, Aldisio walked us all over the farm so the kids could see the animals one last time. My son AJ was in heaven. I was again blown away by the size of the farm and the amount of food it produced.

One last goodbye to the Salese family at the farm. Here is Aldisio, his son Mirco and me with the kids, who picked some grapes for the road.

They sent us off with a few bottles of their homemade olive oil and a profound appreciation for the strength and determination of a farming family like theirs.

We drove back to Antonella's family and her uncle took us all on a really nice tour of a local castle in Avella. We took in beautiful views of the region and took some great final photos in Italy.

We then went back to the apartment building where we had our last supper in Italy—and it couldn't have been a better one. Antonella's aunt (who is a brilliant cook) quickly threw together what ended up being one of the tastiest meals of our stay in Italy.

She made pepper and eggplant dishes that were to die for. She put out a platter of mozzarella di bufala with beautiful green olives. Then, the sleeper, she started frying eggs and putting them on the table, a few at a time. I vividly remember eating an egg over the peppers with some mozzarella.

"Oh man," I thought, "how hard will it be adjusting back to life in New Jersey?"

We had to wake the kids up the next morning at about 3 a.m. to get to the airport. Somehow, we made it on time and caught the first of two flights headed back to New Jersey. The trip back passed in a blur; "I can't believe it's over," and "I can't believe we did that," raced through my mind.

I didn't realize during the trip (or even en route back to the U.S.) how much this trip would change my life; but it would, dramatically.

The Beginning, or the End?

I can't believe we are back in New Jersey. I can't believe we spent 40 days in Italy.

As I stand here in my kitchen in New Jersey, I realize how much I already miss Italy.

I miss Maria Rosa, and Aldiso, and Nunzia, and Francy. I miss them all—but then I realize something. This isn't the end of a trip to Italy; it is the beginning of a relationship with my Italian relatives. A relationship that me and my family here in the U.S. will be able to build and enjoy for the rest of our lives.

It is a beginning, not an end.

Standing in my kitchen in New Jersey
August 2016

Back Home in New Jersey

We arrived safely back home to New Jersey; for the first week back, I think we all struggled. Late nights, fresh food, and hearing the beautiful language of our ancestors had become the norm for us over the last 40 days in Italy and, oh, how we missed it.

While all of our sightseeing in Le Cinque Terre, Pisa, Rome, and so on were amazing, what I kept thinking about and missing the most was la mia famiglia—my family.

Aldisio, who would walk our kids all over their farm as much as they wanted him to, even in the dead heat of the Italian summer.

Maria Rosa, who went out of her way to make us comfortable and really connect with our children, including taking us out for gelato made from the milk of a buffalo—buono!

Antonio Fasano and his family, who welcomed us into the small village of Controne with open arms, and made sure we all saw the street where my great-grandfather Antonio Fasano was born.

Francy and her family in Sortino, who treated us like we were family they had known forever—because, in some ways, we were.

Nunzia, who treated us all like we were her long-lost children, just returned from a long trip away.

The Beginning, or the End?

It would take some time to get adjusted back to life in New Jersey—but even when we did, we would never forget this trip, and never forget where we came from.

My cousin Francy and I in Sicily.
The beginning of a beautiful relationship.

What We Have Created

Soon after we returned, I recorded episode 23 of *The Italian American Podcast*, titled "Finding Relatives in Italy and Connecting the Italian and American Sides of Your Family." In the episode, my co-host Dolores and I talked about the bond that was created between my Italian and

American families on this trip. It was a bond that will forever thrive, as long as we continue to nurture it.

Think about it—before this entire experience, we had only heard about where our family came from and that we had living relatives somewhere in Italy. Now, we had so much more than that. We had the photos, the experiences, and the relationships to prove it.

My children will always know exactly where they came from because they have seen the towns—and I know we will all be back there very soon.

Your Time is Now

As much as I wrote this book for my family to remember our trip, I also wrote it for you. I believe that every Italian American can follow the steps laid out in Part I of this book to find their family (or at least information about their family).

Whether or not you have living relatives in Italy, I highly recommend that you attempt to find out what villages your ancestors came from and visit these places.

Then, when someone asks you, "What nationality are you?" or "Where in Italy is your family from?", rather than saying, "Italian,", or saying "Naples," or "Sicily," you will have the opportunity to say so much more.

When you think about your life and the meaning behind it, your place of origin is a critical part of your story. It is my hope that this book can help you write

The Beginning, or the End?

that part of your own story now. But remember, it's only the beginning; once you write the beginning of your story, it can continue to get more exciting from there.

Please keep in touch with me through the website for this book, FortyDaysInItaly.com, where I will post some more photos. I want to hear your story. There is also a special travel planning document that you can use to plan your trip on the book website.

It doesn't matter how old you are—discovering where you came from is an introduction to a whole new world. It's the beginning, not the end.

A presto!

Acknowledgments

I would like to express my gratitude to the many people who helped me turn my summer in Italy into a memory that can be treasured forever through this book; thank you to all those who provided support, talked things over, read, wrote, offered comments, and assisted in the editing, proofreading and design.

Above all, I want to thank my family (in both Italy and the U.S.), who supported and encouraged me in spite of all the time it took to work on this project.

Last and not least, I would like to thank you, the reader. A book is not a book without someone to read it, and I am honored you have decided to do so.

This book may be just the beginning of your journey. Please visit the book website at FortyDaysInItaly.com to take the next step.

About the Author

Anthony Fasano is a proud Italian American whose family comes from both the regions of Campania and Sicilia. Anthony's professional background is in engineering. He started his career in civil engineering, but has since transitioned into coaching and training for engineers.

He has created several successful content brands and podcasts including "The Engineering Career Coach Podcast," which has been downloaded over one million times. He has also created "The Civil Engineering Podcast," and of course most recently, his favorite, "The Italian American Podcast."

Fasano has authored several books including a self-published book for engineers entitled *Engineer Your Own Success*, which was picked up by Wiley Press, as well as a series of children's books which he co-authored with his now 10-year-old daughter, titled *Purpee the Purple Dragon*. They have delivered hundreds of copies of the books to pediatric cancer centers around the United States.

You can find Fasano's latest Italian American related projects, including all episodes of The Italian American Podcast, at ItalianAmericanExperience.com.

Learn More at

FortyDaysInItaly.com

www.ingramcontent.com/pod-product-compliance
Lightning Source LLC
Chambersburg PA
CBHW032222010526
44113CB00032B/290